KABUKI DEMOCRACY

ALSO BY ERIC ALTERMAN

Why We're Liberals:
A Handbook to Restoring America's Most Important Ideals
(Viking, 2008, Penguin, 2009)

When Presidents Lie:
A History of Official Deception and Its Consequences
(Viking, 2004, Penguin, 2005)

The Book on Bush:
How George W. (Mis)Leads America.
(Viking, 2004, Penguin, 2005 co-author)

What Liberal Media?
The Truth About Bias and the News
(Basic, 2003, 2004)

It Ain't No Sin To Be Glad You're Alive:
The Promise of Bruce Springsteen
(Little, Brown & Co, 1999, Back Bay, 2001)

Who Speaks for America?
Why Democracy Matters in Foreign Policy
(Cornell University Press, 1998)

Sound and Fury:
The Making of the Punditocracy.
(HarperCollins, 1992, 1993, and Cornell University Press, 2000)

KABUKI DEMOCRACY

The System vs. Barack Obama

ERIC ALTERMAN

NATION
BOOKS

NEW YORK

Published by Nation Books, A Member of the Perseus Books Group

Nation Books is a co-publishing venture of the Nation Institute and the Perseus Books Group

Books published by Nation Books are available at special discounts for bulk purchases in the United States by corporations, institutions, and other organizations. For more information, please contact the Special Markets Department at the Perseus Books Group, 2300 Chestnut Street, Suite 200, Philadelphia, PA 19103, or call (800) 810-4145, ext. 5000, or e-mail special.markets@perseusbooks.com.

Editorial production by the Book Factory
Design by Cynthia Young in Adobe Garamond Pro

Cataloging-in-Publication Data is available at the Library of Congress
ISBN: 9781568586595

10 9 8 7 6 5 4 3 2 1

To my father, Carl Alterman,
in his eightieth year on the planet and his fiftieth year as my dad,
with deepest gratitude and admiration.

CONTENTS

You've Got a Lot of
Nerve To Say You Are My Friend

Few liberals or progressives would take issue with the argument that, significant accomplishments notwithstanding, the Obama presidency has been a big disappointment. As Mario Cuomo famously observed, candidates campaign in poetry but govern in prose. And, yes, the achievements are, when judged in comparison with those of his immediate predecessors, undeniably impressive. There are health care reform, financial reform, the economic stimulus, tobacco regulation, student loan reform, credit card reform, and equal pay, all of which unarguably put Barack Obama in the company of Lyndon Johnson and Franklin Delano Roosevelt as one of the most consequential Democratic presidents of the last hundred years. Yet when one examines the fine print on these bills, it becomes equally undeniable that Obama voters have been asked to accept some awfully "prosaic" compromises.

This turn of events is particularly disheartening when one recalls the powerful wave of progressive support Obama rode to the White House, coupled with the near total discrediting of his conservative Republican opposition, owing to the disastrous consequences of George Bush's presidency. In order to pass his health care legislation, for instance, Obama was required to specifically repudiate his pledge to prochoice voters to "make preserving women's rights under *Roe v. Wade* a priority as president." That promise apparently was lost in the same drawer as his insistence that "any [health care reform] plan I sign must include an insurance exchange . . . including a public option." Labor unions were among candidate Obama's most fervent and dedicated foot soldiers, and many were no doubt inspired by his pledge "to fight for the passage of the Employee Free Choice Act." Yet that act appears deader than Jimmy Hoffa. Environmentalists were no doubt steeled through the frigid days of New Hampshire canvassing by Obama's promise that "as president, I will set a hard cap on all carbon emissions at a level that scientists say is necessary to curb global warming—an 80 percent reduction by 2050." But that goal appears to have gone up the chimney in thick black smoke. And remember when Obama promised, right before the election, to "put in place the common-sense regulations and rules of the road I've been calling for since March—rules that will keep our market free, fair and honest; rules that will restore accountability and responsibility in our corporate boardrooms"? Neither, apparently, does he. Indeed, if one examines the gamut of legislation passed and executive orders issued that relate to the promises made by candidate Obama, one can only wince at the slightly hyperbolic joke made by late-night comedian Jimmy Fallon, who quipped that the president's goal appeared to be to "finally deliver on the campaign promises made by John McCain."

None of us know what lies inside the president's heart. It is at least possible that he fooled gullible progressives during the election into believing he was a left-liberal partisan when in fact he is much closer to a conservative corporate shill. An awful lot of progressives, including two I happen to know who sport Nobel Prizes on their shelves, feel this way, and their perspective cannot be completely discounted. The Beltway view of Obama, meanwhile, posits just the opposite. That view—insistently repeated, for instance, by the *Wall Street Journal's* nonpartisan, nonideological news columnist Gerald Seib—is that the president's problem is that he and his allies in the Democratic Party "just overplayed their hand in the last year and a half, moving policy too far left, sparking an equal and opposite reaction in the rightward direction." (Obama's biggest mistake, seconded the *Atlantic Monthly's* Clive Crook, was his failure to "repudiate the left" and "make it [his] enemy.") And Newt Gingrich, speaking from what is actually considered by these same Beltway types as the responsible center of the Republican Party, calls Obama "the most radical president in American history," operating on the basis of "Kenyan, anti-colonial behavior"; Gingrich urges his minions to resist the president's "secular, socialist machine."

My own views remain in flux—subject to adjustment depending on the circumstances. I began the Obama presidency tending toward the view, expressed by young, conservative *New York Times* columnist Ross Douthat, that Barack Obama is a "liberal who's always willing to cut a deal and grab for half the loaf. He has the policy preferences of a progressive blogger, but the governing style of a seasoned Beltway wheeler-dealer." During the presidential campaign Barack Obama bravely praised Ronald Reagan for having put forth bold ideas that "changed the trajectory of American politics." But as president, Obama chose to work for whatever deal might already be on the table, relying instead on the philosophy of one his early Chicago mentors, Denny Jacobs, who told Obama biographer David Remnick, "Sometimes you can't get the whole hog, so you take the ham sandwich." Even allowing for this orientation on the part of the president, and admitting that from a philosophical standpoint it's one I largely share, I cannot argue that I see the wisdom of all of the compromises he has so far agreed to embrace.

For instance, as a liberal who believes in the power of public rhetoric, I deeply regret Obama's decision to turn dealmaker overnight as he assumed the presidency. I'll admit that this cynic's heart was stirred in ways I never imagined when Obama took the stage in Denver that late summer night in 2008 and summoned up our best angels after eight years of the fear-mongering and dumbed-down divisiveness we

experienced under George Bush. But the fellow who, during the crucial moment in the campaign, asked supporters to join him in com-
mitting themselves to a vision of "A nation healed. A world repaired.
An America that believes again . . . " disappeared inside the Oval
Office on January 20, 2010, never to be seen again. Had the president
been willing to make a stronger case for his core beliefs from the bully
pulpit, his words might have had a salutary effect on the tone of
American politics just as John F. Kennedy's did during his presidency,
despite a similar commitment to a dealmaker's style of politics. Many
people were inspired by Kennedy to do great things even if the president himself saw the need for political compromise whenever necessary. It almost certainly would have been beneficial to Obama's
youthful supporters, who turned out in greater numbers than ever before and in greater margins for a Democratic candidate but never got
to hear the values he professed as candidate given voice by the president they helped to elect. Perhaps an Obama who emulated Ronald
Reagan and sought to move the rhetorical center of American politics
back to a more humane, progressive place would have generated a
more humane, progressive political conversation in this country.
Surely, it would have been worth a try. But as much as I may regret
Obama's decision to forego this option and throw himself into dealmaking, I cannot in good conscience argue that had President Obama
been more Reaganesque in his rhetoric, the result would necessarily
have been the passage of better, more progressive legislation. For the
truth, dear reader, is that it does not much matter who is right about
what Barack Obama dreams of in his political imagination. Nor are
the strategic mistakes made by the Obama team really all that crucial,
except perhaps at the margins of any given policy. The far more important fact for progressive purposes is simply this: The system is
rigged, and it's rigged against us.

Sure, presidents can pretty easily pass tax cuts for the wealthy
and powerful corporations. They can start whatever wars they wish

and wiretap whomever they want without warrants. They can order the torture of terrorist suspects, lie about it, and see that their intelligence services destroy the evidence. But what they cannot do, even with supermajorities in both houses of Congress behind them, is pass the kind of transformative progressive legislation that Barack Obama promised in his 2008 presidential campaign. The chapters that follow explain why.

CHAPTER ONE

When the Autumn Weather
Turns the Leaves to Flame

The American political system is nothing if not complicated, and so, too, are the reasons for its myriad points of democratic dysfunction. Some are endemic to our constitutional regime and all but impossible to address save by the extremely cumbersome (and profoundly unlikely) prospect of amending the Constitution. Others are the result of a corrupt capital culture that likes it this way and has little incentive to change. Many are the result of the peculiar commercial and ideological structure of our media, which not only frame our political debate but also determine which issues will be addressed. A few are purely functions of the politics of the moment or just serendipitous bad luck. And if we really mean to change things, instead of just complaining about them, it behooves us to figure out which of these choke points can be opened up and which cannot. For if our politicians cannot keep the promises they make as candidates, then our commitment to political democracy becomes a kind of Kabuki exercise; it resembles a democratic process at great distance but mocks its genuine intentions in substance.

We live, as the late historian Tony Judt once wrote, in an "age of forgetting," and nowhere is this truer than in our political discourse. Rarely do we stop to remind ourselves that, as a *New York Times* editorial put it, Obama "took office under an extraordinary burden of problems created by President George W. Bush's ineptness and blind ideology." Clear environmental threats had been allowed to fester. The Bush Justice Department was engaged in what appears to have been widespread criminal action in a host of areas. We were fighting two wars, hamstrung by the hatred of most of the world's citizens, and operating torture centers (and lying about it) across the globe. What's more, based on the theory of the "unitary executive," George Bush and Dick Cheney were claiming near dictatorial powers to ignore both houses of Congress and even the courts when it suited their purposes. According to the September 2010 calculations of Nobel laureate economist Joseph Stiglitz (writing with Linda J. Bilmes), the economic cost of Bush's foolish Iraq misadventure was well over $3 trillion, and this does not begin to account for its humanitarian, strategic, diplomatic, constitutional, institutional, and moral costs as well. Meanwhile, the economic condition of the nation left to Barack Obama was the worst any president had seen since the Great Depression. Author Thomas Edsall observes, "The price of Bush's dereliction was immense," as "more than 8.4 million jobs were lost and nearly three million homes were foreclosed on, with more to come. The number of personal and commercial bankruptcies reached unprecedented levels. In 2008—a single year—American households lost $11 trillion, 18 percent of their wealth." On the fiscal side, Edsall calculates, under this allegedly conservative president,

> federal spending rose from 18.5 percent of GDP [gross domestic product] in 2001 to 21 percent in 2008, while a $125.3 billion surplus became a $364.4 billion deficit. Median family income, which had grown from $42,429 in 1980 to $46,049 in 1990, and which grew again during the Clinton Administration to $50,557 by 2000, shrank under George W. Bush, standing at $50,223 in 2007 before the start of the recession. During the Bush presidency, three million jobs were created. That compares to 23.1 million during

Bill Clinton's two terms, and 16 million during Ronald Reagan's. That's the lowest level of job creation of any post–World War II president.

Barack Obama could hardly have been more accurate than on February 7, 2010, when, speaking of health care reform, he told a CBS News interviewer, "Getting something passed through Congress with 535 members is hard." And as president, he had no choice but to "play the cards [he was] dealt." But how, exactly? Put yourself in President Obama's shoes on January 21, 2009. Should he allow the deficit to explode or the economy to implode? Should he bail out the banks? Nationalize them? Break them up? Allow Detroit to die? Invite the firing of tens, possibly hundreds of thousands of teachers, police, firefighters, and emergency workers by state and local governments strapped by falling tax revenues? Should he close Guantánamo and Bagram prisons? End rendition? Get out of Iraq? Reverse signing statements? Outlaw domestic spying? Cut carbon emissions? And by the way, exactly how would he accomplish these things—and simultaneously? By legislation? By executive fiat? By magic? Believe me, I could go on.

America's most irresponsible, incompetent, and ideologically obsessed presidency not only left most of these political and economic crises on its successor's plate; it also often masked significant problems that received virtually no attention, so prominent were the myriad crises it caused. Many of these are more worrisome than the ones that made the front page. We all knew of the Bush administration's incompetence in the realm of economic policy, as its inability/refusal to police the financial industry led directly to the worst economic crisis the world had seen since the Great Depression, a performance that mirrored the combination of incompetence, malfeasance, dishonesty, and corruption that resulted in the spectacularly counterproductive invasion and occupation of Iraq. And its commitment to the exploitation and despoilment of the environment was no secret to those who paid at least a modicum of attention to the news.

But what of the rest of the Bush administration's responsibilities—the ones that never made the front page? Remember, entitlements were rising unsustainably; so, too, was America's exploding foreign debt to China. Our education system was falling farther and farther behind that of other Western nations as "No Child Left Behind" succeeded largely in increasing our students' ability to take tests. And, largely ignored by the media, much of our physical infrastructure had corroded to the point of near collapse. Mass transit systems were being shut down in localities across the country owing to a lack of funds to pay for them. School buildings were being closed without adequate replacement because of unsafe infrastructural conditions. Streetlights in some places, including the conservative bastion of Colorado Springs, Colorado, were being shut off at night.

According to the American Society of Civil Engineers, "More than 26%, or one in four, of the nation's bridges are either structurally deficient or functionally obsolete," a problem that would likely cost roughly $17 billion per year to repair, or almost twice what has been budgeted. One-third of America's major roads are, the engineers tell us, "in poor or mediocre condition and 45 percent of major urban highways are congested." Drinking water systems "face an annual shortfall of at least $11 billion to replace aging facilities." Inland waterways, wastewater systems, and levees: All of these crucial systems rate a "D" or lower. What's more, this neglect at the federal level is matched by an equal lack of interest in these topics by the mainstream media. A valuable study by Jodi Enda in the *American Journalism Review* reveals an appalling apathy with regard to these issues on the part of virtually every major news organization.

The result of this malign neglect is that post-Bush America is one disaster after another waiting to happen, all of which—when they do—are laid at the feet of the current president, regardless of whether addressing them is consistent with his policy agenda. For if he does not find a way to do so, they will likely overwhelm it. The financial crisis that dominated Obama's early months—and almost brought down the entire world economy—is one obvious example. Afghanistan and Iraq are another. But let's consider for a moment the crisis that most pundits termed to be the most significant of Obama's early presidency: the BP oil spill in the Gulf of Mexico that began on April 15, 2010. President Obama was, naturally, responsible for his administration's reaction to the spill as well as his ill-considered decision, taken just weeks before the spill, to allow expanded drilling in coastal areas. But most mainstream media reporters viewed the oil spill as an act of God or of individual corporate negligence. But when the *Wall Street Journal*'s Peggy Noonan published a column during the final weekend of May in which she mused that she could not "see how the president's position and popularity can survive the oil spill," she appeared to argue that the mistakes made by the Obama administration in the wake of the disaster somehow constituted the entire story, at least insofar as it allowed pundits and the public to judge his success as president. In fact, the conditions that led to the spill—including the egregious malfeasance that empowered BP and the rest of the industry to ignore the most basic precautions—were a direct outgrowth of the Bush/Cheney industry-friendly defenestration of the government's basic regulatory functions.

As the *American Journalism Review* study notes, before the spill occurred, not a single editor or producer thought to call a reporter and say, "Hey, why not take a look at what's up over at the Minerals Management Service?" (The MMS, located inside the Department of Interior, manages the nation's natural gas, oil, and other mineral resources on the country's outer continental shelf.) Virtually nothing had been written about the MMS at all of late, save for an infamous four-year sex scandal. According to MMS spokesman Nicholas Pardi, before the BP oil spill not a single reporter in the country covered the service's activities full time. And yet in the wake of this endless disaster, we've learned, for instance, that the MMS did not require oil companies to install reliable backup systems to trigger blowout preventers in case of an emergency. No enforcement mechanisms existed at all. During the Bush years, regulators allowed the oil executives to fill in their own inspection reports in pencil, which were merely traced over before their official submission. Free hunting and fishing trips, tickets to games, and expensive meals were the norm at the Lake Charles office, all provided by the oil companies. Taking such gifts "appears to have been a generally accepted practice," according to the department's acting inspector general, Mary L. Kendall. One MMS employee undertook four inspections of platforms while in the process of negotiating the terms of his employment with that same company. Another was suspected of using crystal meth during his inspections. It's no wonder that that the MMS collected only sixteen fines from the more than 400 investigations of Gulf of Mexico drilling incidents during the previous five years. The agency found roughly 200 violations of its regulations but showed virtually no interest in pursuing any of them.

Meanwhile, as a result of this almost comically lax enforcement, BP executives felt no compunction about ignoring those safety and environmental rules to which it was legally subject. One 2001 report found that the company paid little attention to the safety equipment that it would need in the event of an emergency shutdown. It often fell back on the least expensive and less than reliable deepwater well design and did so far more frequently than its industry competitors. At the well where the explosion took place, numerous workers also voiced concerns about poor equipment reliability, "which they believed was as a result of drilling priorities taking precedence over planned maintenance," according to a survey commissioned by the rig's owner, Transocean. Despite these findings, nearly half the workers surveyed feared potential reprisals if they raised their voices. Any number of key components—including the blowout preventer rams and failsafe valves of the rig—went uninspected over a period of more than nine years, although the company's guidelines called for them to be evaluated every three to five years. But a number of workers entered false data owing to what many of them viewed as the company's "counterproductive" safety system. Another BP internal investigation found 390 overdue maintenance problems with the rig a month before the spill began, though to be honest, we may never know the full story. As late as October 2010, Transocean was still refusing to cooperate with the federally appointed panel investigating the disaster and would not turn over key materials related to its compliance with international safety management codes. It also declined to provide testimony from a key manager called by the panel as a witness.

Investigators did, however, garner sufficient data to determine that all of these actions were undoubtedly part of a larger pattern within BP, Transocean, and many, if not most, of the contractors that worked on the well. Another report, from 2004, discovered a pattern of company intimidation toward employees who expressed uneasiness about safety or environmental practices. California officials accused the company of falsifying its 2002 fuel tank inspections, adding that four of five of its storage facilities failed to meet proper standards. BP was forced to settle a lawsuit brought by the South Coast Air Quality Management District for more than $100 million. In 2005 a Texas City refinery explosion cost fifteen lives, owing in part to a failed warning system that one report found consistent with practices at "all five U.S. refineries, not just Texas City." Incredibly, during the very days, early April 2010, when the world was focusing on the spill in the Gulf of Mexico, a BP refinery in Texas City, Texas, released huge amounts of toxic chemicals into the air for forty days in a row; these toxins went unnoticed by residents and unaddressed by BP until local area children began experiencing respiratory problems. According to one report, a total of 538,000 pounds of toxic chemicals, including the carcinogen benzene, escaped into the atmosphere. And instead of shutting the refinery down, the company merely diverted gases to a smokestack and tried to burn them off, allowing hundreds of thousands of pounds more to contaminate the air. Moreover, BP did not alert local officials to the danger until the contamination was complete.

It was therefore a surprise only in the specifics of the action itself, rather than the overall pattern of malign neglect, when we learned in the first official finding of responsibility for the blowout that Dick Cheney's old firm, Halliburton, had conducted three separate laboratory experiments demonstrating that its cement mixture—the mixture that apparently set the explosion off in the first place—repeatedly tested as inferior to industry standards, and yet, as the panel's lead investigator, Fred H. Bartlit Jr., explains, "There is no indication that Halliburton highlighted to BP the significance of the foam stability data or that BP personnel raised any questions about it."

Given all of these derelictions, and much more besides, *New York Times* pundit Paul Krugman is quite right to point out that the failures of both the MMS and BP that led to the spill—MMS's failure "to require a backup shutdown system that is standard in much of the rest of the world, even though its own staff declared such a system necessary," the exemption the service gave BP "from the requirement that they file plans to deal with major oil spills," and its allowing "BP to drill Deepwater Horizon without a detailed environmental analysis"— are part of a pattern relevant not just to the Bush/Cheney administration's lackadaisical approach to environmental regulation. Rather, they also reflect the entire Bush administration's attitude toward governance in general and regulation in particular. "For the Bush administration was, to a large degree, run by and for the extractive industries," Krugman notes. Its appointees were not merely corporate lobbyists and shills who frequently possessed little interest and less competence in the areas they were being asked to regulate. They were often also corrupt. Again to take just one of many potential examples, the Bush/Cheney deputy secretary of the interior (the man credited with actually running the place) was former coal industry lobbyist J. Steven Griles, who in 2007 had pled guilty to lying to Congress about his ties to Jack Abramoff's criminal operations. (Abramoff, once a high-powered, well-connected Republican lobbyist, pled guilty in 2006 to three criminal felony counts as a result of various acts of fraud and corruption, many of which involved massive amounts of money being paid out by Indian tribes and ending up in the pockets of Abramoff, his associates, and powerful Republican politicians.)

As it happens, Cheney himself was crucial in creating these conditions. Dick Cheney's National Energy Policy Task Force concluded in May 2001 that many of the protections under which drillers had previously operated were no longer necessary, as new, allegedly more "efficient drilling and production methods" could "reduce emissions; practically eliminate spills from offshore platforms; and enhance worker safety, lower risk of blowouts, and provide better protection of groundwater resources."

Josh Dorner of the Center for American Progress observes that one of the worst elements of what has come to be known as the "Dick Cheney Energy Bill" had a direct role in eliminating the kind of regulatory oversight that may have prevented the blowout of BP's Mississippi Canyon 252 well on April 20 of this year. Section 390 of the legislation dramatically expanded the circumstance under which drilling operations could forego environmental reviews and be approved almost immediately under so-called "categorical exclusions" from the National Environmental Policy Act. The use of such exclusions went on to widespread abuse under the Bush administration. BP's blown-out well did not undergo an environmental review thanks to a categorical exclusion. (BP was lobbying as recently as April [2010] to expand the use of such exclusions.)

Krugman correctly notes that Barack Obama "isn't completely innocent of blame in the current spill," owing to the fact that BP "received an environmental waiver for Deepwater Horizon after Mr. Obama took office." Indeed, as the current deputy interior secretary later mused, "What happened to all the stakeholders—Congress, environmental groups, industry, the government—all stakeholders involved were lulled into a sense of what has turned out to be false security." But the "broader pattern" here, Krugman avers, is one of "the degradation of effective government by antigovernment ideology." As a result of this ideology's ruinous effects, a similar sense of false security about any number of aspects our government's regulatory responsibilities presently permeates our public life. And like an oil gusher spewing its poison into a pristine Louisiana wetland, this politically poisonous legacy of malign neglect has the potential to despoil almost every aspect of President Obama's agenda. But you will rarely, if ever, hear them discussed when it comes time for the president to face the consequences of that agenda. It's as if Bush and Cheney left one time bomb after another and the Obama administration is being held responsible for failing to predict where and when each one will explode.

CHAPTER TWO

Don't Know What I Want
But I Know How to Get It

"The self-critical element of the progressive mind is probably a healthy thing, but it can also be debilitating," Barack Obama told *Rolling Stone* magazine in the fall of 2010. Progressives need to keep this in mind, particularly in light of the amazing series of interlocking challenges that faced Obama's presidency in merely restoring some sensible form of equilibrium to the governance of the United States. What's more, he was attempting to work with a minority party with no strategic stake whatever in sensible governance. When, for instance, the unemployment figure reached 9.5 percent—or, more accurately, 16.5 percent if we include the people who had given up looking—in the summer of 2010, some of the lost jobs could be attributed to the failure of Congress to appropriate funds to replace lost state and local revenue in time for localities to retain their needed staffing levels of police, firefighters, schoolteachers, and the like; a legislative package was purposely delayed in the Senate by a combination of single-senator holds and party-line obstructionist votes. But bad employment numbers were actually good news for Republicans, as they were roundly interpreted as evidence of the failure of the Obama administration's economic policies and therefore increased the likelihood of strong Republican showings in the coming November midterm elections.

As a matter of fact, the worse things got for the country, the better they looked for Republican candidates. And given that Republicans can plausibly claim to be ideologically in sync with just about any nonmilitary budget cut no matter what the ultimate effect, what possible incentive do the Republicans have to cooperate with the Democratic majority to pass legislation that will actually improve economic conditions? The two parties are demonstrably different in this respect. Democrats, even in the minority, participate in solutions designed to improve governance. They cannot help themselves. A commitment to the principle of good governance is the primary reason most Democrats tend toward politics in the first place. One might argue that this faith in government's ability to improve people's lives is misplaced, or that it becomes easily corrupted over time by the temptations of power and privilege, but few serious political observers would deny its initial presence. This is rarely true of Republicans, who are suspicious of government on principle and opposed to successful programs in practice and therefore happy to see government programs fail and, ideally, disappear entirely.

Ironically, given the deeply contested manner in which George W. Bush ascended to the presidency in 2000 despite his second-place finish in the popular vote and a transparent power grab on his behalf by the U.S. Supreme Court, it is Obama's, not Bush's, legitimacy that has come under attack by mainstream Republicans. As environmental reporter Dave Roberts describes it, "At the federal Congressional level, the Republican Party has become tight in its discipline, extreme in its ideology, and utterly unprincipled in its tactics." To be fair to the Democrats, they are a far more ideologically diverse party than the Republicans and contain many moderates, many of who, in past Congresses, would easily have been conservatives. To further complicate matters, the more conservative or "centrist" representatives are almost always the most vulnerable because they do not represent reliably liberal districts (many were recently recruited for the purposes of winning in "purple" districts). As NPR's Ron Elving observed following the publication of yet another poll predicting a Republican landslide, House Democrats were divided between their safe "sitting pretty faction" and "the more fragile 'scaredy cat' faction that could be carried off by even the gentlest of anti-incumbent breezes." As a result, the Democratic leadership in both houses is forever forced to compromise with its own side rather than its opposition. Now add to this the fact that, as Roberts rightly notes, "Congressional Republicans exercise far more party discipline, are far more extreme ideologically, and are far more willing to twist and abuse procedure than are Congressional Democrats." It's true, as pundits like to claim, that both sides "do it," but Republican conservatives do it better, more often, and to far greater effect. As New York congressman Anthony Weiner wryly observes, too often Democrats arrive at "knife fights carrying library books."

Again, to offer just one relatively insignificant example, when Democratic congressman Neil Abercrombie of Hawaii announced his plans to leave Congress to run for governor, he picked as his date of departure February 28, just before the big make-'em-or-break-'em series of votes on health care reform. Barely a week later, Republican congressman Nathan Deal of Georgia made the same announcement regarding his ambition to occupy his state's governor's chair, but his Republican colleagues prevailed upon him to stick around long enough to vote against health care. Meanwhile, and I wish I were making this up, Abercrombie's Democratic colleagues not only let him run away from the fight but also gave him a going-away party. Too bad Abercrombie was already gone. (And in an almost too-fitting ending, the Democrats lost this bluest of blue seats—temporarily at least—in the May special election, owing to their inability to settle on a single candidate in time for the vote.)

Take the example of health care reform, for instance. Clearly, the American health care system demanded an overhaul for reasons of both equity and efficiency. Per capita health spending in the United States had been increasing at nearly twice the rate as that in other wealthy countries; by 2004 U.S. health care spending was two and a half times per citizen that of the median amount for its competitors and far more than any other country as a percentage of gross domestic product (GDP). And what do we get for all our money? Given that about one-third of the spending went into wasteful and counterproductive bureaucratic shuffling and endlessly redundant layers of administration, not nearly as much as one would have had a right to expect. Going into 2009, the United States and South Africa were the only two developed countries in the world that did not provide health care for all of their citizens. Nationally, roughly 30 percent of American children were without health insurance, and it was not unusual for them to receive no checkups or vaccinations for the entire year. The United States ranked eighty-fourth in the world for measles immunizations and eighty-ninth for polio. Childhood-immunization rates in the United States were lower than average. Infant-mortality rates were in the nineteenth percentile of industrialized nations. And children were hardly the only problem. American life expectancy was lower than the Western average. According to the World Health Organization, the United States ranked twenty-eighth in the years its citizens could expect to live healthy lives

Republicans never bothered to come up with an alternative proposal to Obama's health care plan. Actually addressing these issues could hardly have been less relevant to their political agenda. All they needed were the words "socialism," "government takeover," "death panels," and, most of all, "no." ("We're the party of 'Hell, no!'" cried Sarah Palin to a crowd of cheering southern Republicans in April 2010.) When Senator Jim DeMint (R-SC) introduced a GOP stimulus plan, authored by the Heritage Foundation, it consisted in its entirety of making the Bush tax cuts permanent and adding to them additional tax breaks for corporations and wealthy Americans. If enacted—never a serious possibility—this plan would have cost roughly three times what Obama's plan is estimated to cost over the next ten years. Even DeMint found it necessary to admit that the plan was "not innovative or particularly clever. In fact, it's only eleven pages." Republicans stuck to this line throughout Obama's first two years in office, deriding the impact of the stimulus, complaining of out-of-control deficit spending, and yet demanding the retention of the enormously costly Bush tax cuts aimed primarily at the extremely wealthy. They did so despite the fact that the nonpartisan Congressional Budget Office analyzed the short-term effects of eleven potential options for dealing with the present unemployment crisis and found that retaining the Bush tax cuts for the wealthy offered the least powerful "bang for the buck," owing to wealthy people's proclivity to save, rather than spend, additional income. But when on a Fox News Sunday program in late July 2010 Chris Wallace inquired of then-GOP House minority leader, now House Speaker, John Boehner as to whether he was aware that "a number of top economists say what we need is more economic stimulus," the Republican leader replied with apparent pride in his ignorance, "Well, I don't need to see GDP numbers or to listen to economists. All I need to do is listen to the American people, because they've been asking the question now for eighteen months, 'Where are the jobs?'"

At the same time, Republican leadership in both houses continued to insist that the extension of the Bush tax cuts would magically pay for itself. (As Senate minority leader Mitch McConnell told one reporter in July 2010, "There's no evidence whatsoever that the Bush tax cuts actually diminished revenue. They increased revenue, because of the vibrancy of these tax cuts in the economy.") But by this time this argument had been repudiated by the experience of the previous thirty years, during which deficits exploded under the tax-cutting policies of Presidents Ronald Reagan and George H. W. Bush, and by the judgments of virtually every single reputable economist in America, including Republican economists. These latter included

Greg Mankiw, George W. Bush's chair of the Council of Economic Advisers from 2003 to 2005 ("Some supply-siders like to claim that the distortional effect of taxes is so large that increasing tax rates reduces tax revenue. Like most economists, I don't find that conclusion credible for most tax hikes"); Andrew Samwick, chief economist at the council from 2004 to 2005 ("No thoughtful person believes that this possible offset [from the Bush tax cuts] more than compensated for the first effect for these tax cuts. Not a single one"); Ed Lazear, chair of the council in 2007 ("I certainly would not claim that tax cuts pay for themselves"); and Hank Paulson, President Bush's secretary of the Treasury ("As a general rule, I don't believe that tax cuts pay for themselves").

This myopia was, to no one's surprise, much in evidence in the 2010 Republican election document, "Pledge to America," amid all the lip-service paid to deficit reduction and fiscal responsibility in the face of Washington's "out of control spending." But as the policy-minded blogger and columnist Ezra Klein observed on the day the document was published, "The two most consequential policies in the proposal are the full extension of the Bush tax cuts and the full repeal of the health-care law. The first would increase the deficit by more than $4 trillion over the next 10 years, and many trillions of dollars more after that. The second would increase the deficit by more than $100 billion over the next 10 years, and many trillions of dollars more after that. Nothing in the document comes close to paying for these two proposals."

The self-contradiction never stops. The Republicans solemnly announce that "small business must have certainty that the rules won't change every few months" and then go on to propose the "repeal and replace[ment] of the government takeover of health care" (including its cost-containment provisions) with a new and hitherto unmentioned policy whose "rules" are nowhere available (and, one guesses, never will be). Ditto the called-for reductions in funding for Fannie

Mae and Freddie Mac, which would have enormous effects on the housing market, though, alas, entirely unpredictable ones. And because the debate is focused entirely on what the Obama administration has been able to accomplish to jump-start the economy, the purposeful impediments of Republicans in Congress, together with the other-worldliness of the putative "solutions" they propose, are barely mentioned in the political debate that surrounds the question.

This phenomenon is replicated with regard to foreign policy, where, if anything, Obama has been an even greater disappointment to liberals than on domestic policy, owing to his willingness to embrace Bush-era policies on rendition and secrecy, his refusal to close Guantánamo or Bagram prisons, and his decision not to rethink his earlier commitment to doubling down on Bush's commitment to defend a corrupt order in both Afghanistan and Pakistan. And yet how is he described by Republican leaders for these concessions? As Republican House whip Eric Cantor informed a Heritage Foundation audience in May 2010, America's defenses are "hemorrhaging" because Obama's "policies bespeak a naive moral relativism in which the United States bears much responsibility for the problems we face around the world." This from a politician who enthusiastically supported the Bush administration's illegal torture of suspected terrorists and attempted suspension of habeas corpus for accused American citizens.

Anyone who observes the current state of the Republican Party, whether at the elite or the grassroots level, will not find much clamoring for powerful public policy proposals. The "Pledge to America" promises to "fully fund missile defense" without mentioning that, despite countless billions spent on the project since Ronald Reagan originally proposed it a generation ago, missile defense has never been found to work in any meaningful fashion. (The fiscal responsibility issue rears its head again.) But what the congressional Republicans lack in seriousness, however, they make up in self-discipline, particularly when compared to the constantly divided (and frequently dispirited)

Democrats. Republicans, unlike Democrats, are able to keep their members united in party-line votes at least in part because conservatives enjoy a genuine political movement that is eager to challenge incumbents in primary contests should they stray from the fold. Liberal Democrats, in contrast, have no such enforcement mechanism and hence no ability to threaten deviants and turncoats seeking to save their own political skin.

The combination of increased radicalization and willful ignorance of the postelection Republican base provides yet another roadblock to systemic cooperation. In August 2010, 40 percent of Republicans could not, for certain, identify the country in which Barack Obama had been born and 46 percent said they were pretty sure their president was a Muslim. Whatever his religion, more than 50 percent of Republicans surveyed believed it to be either "definitely true" or "probably true" that Obama "sympathizes with the goals of fundamentalists who want to impose Islamic law around the world." Barely a third disagreed. Now, combine this with the party's historic ideological antipathy toward government solutions to societal problems, and you end up with a leadership with no interest whatever in bipartisan legislation. A week after Barack Obama's assumption of office, the American Enterprise Institute's Norm Ornstein noted, "A week into his presidency House Republicans voted unanimously against Obama's move to save the country as it teetered at the edge of deflation and depression—and their leaders danced a victory jig." Senator DeMint famously promised that health care reform could be used to "break" the president. Entirely irrelevant to anyone's calculations, apparently, was the fact that this nasty, big government, end-our-freedoms communistic takeover of the entire health care industry was actually remarkably similar to a plan offered by a Republican senator, John Chafee, in 1993 when his party was complaining (and successfully stymieing) the plan put forth by Bill and Hillary Clinton. And the Troubled Asset Relief Program, against which so many Republicans campaigned even though it was originally designed and voted on during the Bush administration, earned $25.2 billion on its investment of $309 billion in banks and insurance companies and ended up returning taxpayers 8.2 percent over two years, a far higher profit than they could have made buying thirty-year Treasury bonds or just about any other fixed-income investment. Again, so what?

Analysts make a mistake when they discuss these issues as if the facts mattered. According to Republican-until-recently Arlen Specter, long before the White House had offered any details about the bill's content, before even "the ink was dry on the oath of office," the Republican caucus was plotting how to defeat Obama in 2012. Or as Representative Mike Conaway (R-TX), a member of the Republican Steering Committee, put it, "I think, in the minority, you're not responsible for governing" and hence "you can be a little purer in your ideology than when you're trying to get things done." Any president who is committed to legislating in a bipartisan manner is naturally going to be forced to make compromises that many of his supporters find painful. But a president who is dealing with an opposition party uninterested in compromise and answerable only to a constituency driven by ignorance, animus, and prejudice cannot hope to achieve these aims without at least a recognition of the nature of his opposition. It was allegedly Sun Tzu, who warned in *The Art of War*, "If you know yourself but not your enemy, for every victory gained you will also suffer a defeat." Whether by flaw or by design, both Barack Obama and most members of the media covering Washington politics proved awfully slow, more than two thousand years later, admitting these essential facts.

CHAPTER THREE

If That's All There Is, My Friend, Then Let's Keep Dancing

Whatever the motivation, it is has become easier and easier for a determined minority to throw sand in the gears of the legislative process. America's system of political representation, now more than two centuries old, has grown ever more anachronistic. For instance, when the U.S. Senate was created, the most populous state had just twelve times more people than the least populous one. Now that number is seventy times, giving those in small and underpopulated states a massive political advantage over the rest of us. (Wyoming's two senators each represent 272,000 people; California's, 18,481,000 each.) And it just so happens that the best-represented areas of America are also the most conservative. So when in late September 2010 forty Republican senators elected to block debate on a measure, recommended by President Barack Obama, Secretary of Defense Robert M. Gates, and Chairman of the Joint Chiefs of Staff Admiral Mike Mullen, to end the military's seventeen-year "Don't Ask, Don't Tell" policy regarding gays serving in the military, these senators represented barely 33 percent of the U.S. population. Under current Senate rules, it is actually possible for senators representing just 11 percent of the population to prevent the passage of legislation supported by senators representing the other 89 percent (or fifty-nine senators from the thirty most populous states).

This is just the beginning of the problems Americans face in terms of disproportionate representation. The average age of a U.S. senator is sixty-nine, whereas the median age of Americans, according to the most recent census figures, is just over thirty-five. Women are a majority of the U.S. population but only 17 percent of the Senate. Only four senators are African American, Hispanic, or Native American, even though these minorities represent 33 percent of the population. Most senators are also millionaires; most Americans, needless to say, are not. Elderly white male millionaires therefore do quite well when it comes to legislation; underrepresented groups, not so much.

The minority party has myriad means to bottle up legislation, and owing to a breakdown in comity among senators, no special interest is deemed too small or insignificant to keep Republican senators from monkeying up the works. True, American history provides few moments when genuine progressive reform can be said to have proceeded in a smooth manner and without serious obstacle. Any number of obstructionist techniques have long been available to senators, and virtually every effort to take on powerful interests, no matter how popular the measure in question, must overcome these techniques.

Today, the most common tool of obstruction is a threat to filibuster. In the past, filibusters involved a senator or senators holding forth on the floor of the Senate for days at a time in order to prevent votes on otherwise popular legislation. (Senate laws permit a senator, or a series of senators, to speak for as long as he or she wishes and on any topic unless "three-fifths of the Senators duly chosen and sworn" vote to shut the filibustering senator down.) Genuine filibusters of the kind southern Democrats used to block civil rights legislation in the 1940s and 1950s are largely unknown today; senators find them inconvenient, what with all the back-and-forth travel, fund-raising opportunities, and media appearances an old-style filibuster would cost them. (The average senator spends about 1 percent of his or her time on the floor of the Senate.) But the threat of a filibuster has increased exponentially as the Republicans grow ever more shameless in shutting down votes in which they are in the minority because the inconvenience of an actual filibuster is no longer necessary.

Accurate numbers can be difficult to discern because in most cases the mere threat is enough to win the battle at hand. But if we examine a close corollary—cloture votes—these rose from fewer than ten per (two-year) congressional session during the 1970s to more than a hundred in both the 2006–2008 and 2009–2010 sessions. Political scientist Barbara Sinclair estimates that 70 percent of all Senate bills have been affected by these threats since 2000, nearly ten times the average in the previous century. The same numbers suggest that, even though the Democratic minority under George W. Bush was hardly a paragon of virtue in this respect, the Democrats are still no match for their opponents when it comes to the use and deployment of the body's tactical weaponry of obstruction. Since the Democratic takeover of both houses in 2006, Republicans have more than doubled the 130 cloture motions Democrats had managed to force during the four previous years under George W. Bush.

In yet another fossilized rule left over from the days of stagecoach travel, any senator can freeze any bill merely by placing a personal "hold" on it. This parliamentary procedure allows a single senator to prevent any legislation even from reaching a vote on the Senate floor so long as the party leadership agrees to back him or her (which as a courtesy it usually does). Breaking a hold can be done, but it is an incredibly tedious, time-consuming business, and senators undertake to do it only in extreme circumstances. Meanwhile, parliamentary maneuvers can be put in place to reinstate holds by just two senators who pass them back and forth—called "rolling holds"—and what's more, this maneuver can be done in secret.

Again, Republicans in the 111th Congress proved far more promiscuous in the employment of this antimajoritarian tactic than any before them. As of September 2010, fewer than half of Obama's federal nominees for jobs had been confirmed and 102 out of 854 judgeships remained vacant. Of the 81 judicial nominations Obama sent to the Senate during his first eighteen months in office, only 30 were approved, largely due to single-senator holds placed on individual nominees. As a result, Obama saw fewer than half the number of his nominees approved that George W. Bush had seen approved at the same point in his presidency despite Democratic control of the Senate for the first two years of that presidency. (One judicial nominee was confirmed, following a nine-month Republican hold, by a vote of 99 to 0.) On April 20, 2010, Senator Claire McCaskill (D-MO) took to the floor to try lifting the holds on 56 separate federal nominees. Jon Kyl (R-AZ) objected to every last one of them.

Often, the reasons for a hold have nothing whatever to do with the person or issue in question. Alan Bersin, whose appointment to head the Customs and Border Patrol (CBP) operation (now part of the Department of Homeland Security [DHS]) was stalled until President Obama broke the hold with a series of 15 recess appointments in late March 2010, had been U.S. attorney in California, head of a Justice Department unit overseeing US-Mexico border affairs, head of the San Diego school system, secretary of education for California under Republican governor Arnold Schwarzenegger, and an assistant secretary at DHS. Three CBP commissioners, including two from the Bush administration, asked Republican senators to approve Bersin's appointment, given the significance of the office for which he had been nominated. Why was his appointment not approved by Congress? According to the *Wall Street Journal*, "Senator Charles Grassley (R, Iowa) has raised questions about his personal taxes."

Richard Shelby (R-AL), for another example, placed a "blanket hold" on dozens of nominees over complaints he had involving a Northrop Grumman tanker contract and the construction of a counterterrorism center in his home state. (Another Shelby hold made news in mid-October 2010. Federal Reserve Board of Governors nominee and Massachusetts Institute of Technology professor Peter Diamond was tripped up by Shelby's judgment that he lacked the requisite experience for the position and would be reduced to "learning on the job." The Royal Swedish Academy of Sciences, however, took a different view and awarded Diamond, together with two of his colleagues, the 2010 Nobel Memorial Prize in Economic Science.)

Mary Landrieu (D-LA), meanwhile, insisted on keeping the Office of Management and Budget (OMB) without a director because, while she believed that Obama's nominee, Jack Lew, who had already been cleared by two separate committees, "clearly possesses the expertise necessary to serve as one of the President's most important economic advisors," she said she "found that he lacked sufficient concern for the host of economic challenges confronting the Gulf Coast." Her actual objection was to Obama's refusal to lift a temporary ban on offshore drilling in the area; in an attempt to blackmail the president (of her own party), she ensured that OMB would be without a director as it prepared the government's 2012 budget. (Though to be fair, when Obama did lift the ban in mid-October, Landrieu said she was going to retain her hold for a while in order to "evaluate if today's lifting of the moratorium is actually putting people back to work," before finally lifting it and allowing Lew's confirmation in mid-November 2010.

And the price of these holds does not fall only on the rest of the government. When Kentucky's Jim Bunning—a marvelous pitcher but an awful senator—decided to put a hold on legislation allowing the extension of unemployment benefits, he not only single-handedly caused nearly 1.2 million unemployed workers to lose their benefits; he also caused a furlough of nearly 2,000 Department of Transportation employees without pay, the cutoff of $38 million in project funding for Idaho's Nez Perce National Forest and Fernan Lakes Idaho Panhandle National Forest, and the loss of $86 million for bridge replacements in the Washington, DC, area. And Bunning, who was retiring from office, had zero incentive to allow his colleagues' business to proceed. (Approached by Oregon Democrat Jeff Merkley to see if his genuine concerns might somehow be addressed at less cost to those without work, Senator Bunning replied simply, "Tough shit.")

Americans' natural mistrust of government is an important weapon in the quiver of powerful corporations and wealthy individuals whose freedom of action over the rest of us is enhanced by the weakness of any countervailing power that seeks to regulate them. An October 2010 Kaiser Family Foundation poll that found the percentage who said the country's problems were too big for government to address effectively doubling since the early 1970s was therefore good news indeed for those least in need of help in America. For the current gridlock imposed on Congress by minority obstructionism has had the effect of strengthening the hand of the haves: those with no interest in allowing government to "level the playing field" or even to act effectively in the face of mounting problems no matter how significant or widespread. Rather, as political scientists Jacob H. Hacker and Paul Pierson note, the result of the "slow, quiet, yet inexorable erosion of government's capacity to effectively address the nation's problems" plays into "the hands of those who resist the very idea that government can or should address these big issues—and who understand full well that blocking change in policy yields social and economic outcomes they favor."

Once again, it is incumbent upon liberals and progressives to understand the roots of their current dilemma. The Senate is a drainpipe than can be blocked by the tiniest speck of obstruction. The shamelessness of Obama's opposition in exploiting the system's vulnerability in this respect must be an essential component of any sensible analysis of any progressive president's ability to honor his campaign promises. Exactly why Barack Obama has not done more to illuminate this issue remains, at least to this author, one of the myriad mysteries of the first two years of his presidency.

CHAPTER FOUR

What It Don't Get,
I Can't Use

Political scientists often argue that it is nearly impossible to determine a direct cause-effect connection between a given political
contribution and a vote in Congress. Apologists for the current system of legalized graft—including Chief Justice of the Supreme Court
John Roberts and a single-vote majority of the other justices—will
therefore argue that billions of shareholder dollars are being doled out
by corporations for no apparent purpose. This is, unfortunately, one
of those areas where political science is worse than useless when applied to real life. The nonpartisan Center for Responsive Politics
(CRP) calculated that approximately $3.47 billion was spent lobbying
the federal government in 2009, up from $3.3 billion the previous
year. By the final quarter of the year, lobbies were handing out $20
million a day. The most generous spreaders of wealth were in the
pharmaceutical and health products industries, whose $266.8 million
in 2009 set a record for "the greatest amount ever spent on lobbying
efforts by a single industry for one year," according to CRP. At one
point, PhRMA, the industry-wide trade association, employed forty-
eight lobbying firms, in addition to in-house lobbyists, with a total of
165 people overall, according to the Sunlight Foundation's Paul
Blumenthal. (The Washington D.C.-based Sunlight Foundation
tracks political donations.) PhRMA did not do so because it was

worried about unemployment figures among high-priced lawyers and
ex-lawmakers.

To give just one of perhaps a quadrillion potential examples: In
March 2010 the *New York Times* reported that Senator Bob Corker (R-
TN) had convinced the Senate Banking Committee's chair, Chris
Dodd (D-CT), to remove a provision that would have empowered
federal authorities to crack down on the onerous practices of "payday
lenders." Dodd had planned to give a new consumer protection agency
the power to write and enforce rules governing these friendly fellows
who prey on the poor and those without decent credit ratings—often
U.S. servicemen and -women—with loans sometimes averaging 400
percent annual interest. According to Citizens for Responsibility and
Ethics in Washington, that industry tripled its lobbying budget between 2005 and 2008 to $2.1 million, but the money itself can be dif-
ficult to track. For instance, W. Allan Jones, who started Check into
Cash, in Cleveland, Tennessee, in 1993 and now boasts 1,100 stores in
thirty states, has been what the *Times* calls "a longtime friend and sup-
porter of Mr. Corker's." Jones, his relatives, and his employees have
given Corker's campaign at least $31,000 since 2001, when he ran for
mayor of Chattanooga. Asked whether the industry's campaign contributions to him had shaped his thinking about the issue, Corker
replied, "Categorically, absolutely not." Clearly, the overriding public
interest in having something as inherently sleazy as a barely regulated
payday loan industry must have been Corker's philosophical motivation. (In a denouement that will be familiar to those who closely followed the Democrats' attempt to secure bipartisan support for health
care reform, Corker decided he would not join Dodd in introducing
the legislation, and it became a moot point anyway when the Senate
Banking Committee finally adopted Dodd's own bill on a party-line
vote. That bill allows for a new consumer bureau to enforce the rules it
writes for "nonbank financial companies"—payday lenders included—
over a certain size.)

Corker and the payday loan business are just a microcosm of what happens every day on a vastly larger scale. As of late May 2010 members of the financial committees in both houses had already enjoyed 845 separate fund-raising events, according to the Sunlight Foundation. An analysis by Citizens for Responsibility and Ethics in Washington for the *New York Times* revealed that the fourteen freshmen serving on the House Financial Services Committee raised 56 percent more by mid-2010 in campaign contributions than other freshmen. Party leaders know this, and they place potentially vulnerable members on this committee to aid them with their fund-raising. Naturally, these members are expected to do the industry's bidding there. And it should surprise no one to learn that Senate Energy and Natural Resources Committee members enjoyed an average of $52,000 in campaign contributions from the oil and gas industry in the 2008–2010 election cycle, compared with $24,000 for others in the Senate, according to CRP data.

Financial power need not be justified merely on the basis of the votes it sways. Rather, it can define potential alternatives, invent arguments, inundate with propaganda, and threaten with merely hypothetical opposition. Politicians do not need to "switch" their votes to meet the demands of this money. They can bury bills; they can rewrite the language of bills that are presented; they can convince certain representatives to schedule a golf tournament back home on a day of a key committee vote; they can confuse debate; they can bankroll primary opposition. The manner and means through which money can operate are almost as infinite as its uses in any bordello, casino, or Wall Street brokerage. Just about the only thing money can't buy in politics is love, which is okay because, as Senator David Vitter (R-LA) or ex-Governor Eliot Spitzer (D-NY) can tell you, politics provides plenty of substitutes. As Frank Baumgartner, a political science professor at the University of North Carolina at Chapel Hill and coauthor of the book *Lobbying and Policy Change: Who Wins, Who Loses, and Why*, says,

"The real outcome of most lobbying—in fact, its greatest success—is the achievement of nothing, the maintenance of the status quo. Sixty percent of the time, nothing happens. . . . What we see is gridlock and successful stalemating of proposals, with occasional breakthroughs." And that's just the way the corporate lobbies want it.

Despite Barack Obama's attempts to transform the way business is transacted in Washington, special interest money worked its will through his agenda in Congress to the point where it feels foolish to discuss almost any issue without focusing first on who was buying what from whom. Consider health care. Why was a single-payer program defined as off the table from the proverbial get-go? Why was it impossible to include a public option in the final legislation? Why was the reimportation of prescription drugs declared out of bounds? Why did the insurance industry get to elude antitrust regulations, particularly given the inefficiency with which it delivered its services? Why did it prove impossible simply to lower the age at which Americans became eligible to buy into Medicare? Why wasn't Medicare allowed to negotiate drug prices for seniors in order to secure lower costs? Any of these options would quite likely have lowered the cost of deliverable health care to Americans and significantly increased both the system's reach and its efficiency. The members of the Obama administration working on the issue were undoubtedly aware of all this. And yet they finally presented Congress with legislation that included none of these options. Why?

Well, it wasn't the president's cowardice, shortsightedness, lack of character, or absence of cojones, though many on the left chose to attack Obama in exactly these terms. Without powerful special interests lined up on Obama's side, the battle for reform would have been lost before it had begun. As it was, Obama won by the skin of his teeth.

CAP AND TRADE

The results were far more devastating for the fate of Obama's most significant environmental promise: to curb carbon emissions in the fight against global warming. This was a challenge so significant that even John McCain (R-AZ) once called climate change "a test of foresight, of political courage and of the unselfish concern that one generation owes to the next." The president proposed a complicated cap-and-trade scheme to encourage industry to undertake the necessary reforms. The version that passed in the House could have been read as a gift to certain sectors of the energy and financial industries rather than a serious attempt to control climate-producing emissions. Even so, it was practically communistic in relation to the bill that circulated and ultimately died a deeply deserved death in the Senate, in part as a result of the bad publicity the drilling business received in the wake of the BP oil spill off the Gulf Coast. In the meantime, during the period of negotiation, in order to secure the support of the lobbies deemed sufficiently powerful to kill the bill, its sponsors, John Kerry (D-MA), Joseph Lieberman (I-CT), and on-again-off-again Lindsay Graham (R-SC), were willing to promise the following (according to a detailed report by Ryan Lizza in the *New Yorker*):

- preemption for the U.S. Chamber of Commerce from carbon regulation by the Environmental Protection Agency (EPA) as demanded by the Clean Air Act
- a series of tax incentives for natural gas usage and the creation and installation of natural-gas fueling stations to secure the support of right-wing billionaire T. Boone Pickens
- a special gift to the oil industry regarding the "linked fee" proposal "in exchange for the American Petroleum Institute being quiet" as well as the opening up of "vast portions of the Gulf and the East Coast" to drilling
- $8 billion for the Highway Trust Fund to ensure the support of the South Carolina trucking industry
- "nuclear loan guarantees, an assurance that the cost of carbon would never rise above a certain level, and billions of

dollars' worth of free allowances through 2030" (as well as
preemption by the bill's provisions of those in the Clean Air
Act for electric utilities represented by the Edison Electric
Institute)

As Al Gore observed to Lizza, "The forces wedded to the old patterns
still have enough influence that they were able to use the fear of the
economic downturn as a way of slowing the progress toward this big
transition that we have to make."

Obama's initial cap-and-trade proposal would have put a ceiling
on the amount of carbon to be emitted each year and would have
forced electricity providers and other polluters to purchase permits directly from the government or from each other for their emissions of
greenhouse gases. The system, if successful, would have had the effect
of reducing carbon emissions to 4 percent below 1990 levels by 2020.
This would not, even by administration calculations, have been sufficient to prevent the 2°C temperature rise that a consensus among cli-
matologists insists is the maximum level the planet can sustain without
dire effects taking place. But the cap-and-trade plan was chosen over a
straightforward tax on carbon production in part because it enjoyed
the support of the likes of McCain and of major corporations such as
Shell Oil and Dow Chemical, which stood to profit from it, together
with much of the securities industry, which was eager to create a lucra-
tive market in the buying, selling, and, perhaps, renting of the government's new pollution permits.

This cap-and-trade plan resulted from a lengthy debate over the
various advantages of other market-based regimes. The complex
scheme the plan involved proved more popular to the powerful players
involved than a simple tax on carbon or any of the alternative proposals that produced rewards for citizens with small carbon footprints.
(Although the cap-and-trade mechanism did contain subsidies for the

poor, it offered few benefits or incentives for those whose incomes put them above the poverty level.)

Not so surprisingly, the House bill contained all manner of gifts bestowed by Congress to those with well-funded "government relations" offices. The Peterson Amendment, for instance, named after the chair of the House Agriculture Committee, Collin Peterson (D-MN), exempted big agriculture from many of the emissions standards set by the bill. One can hardly be too shocked to learn that the top three donors to Peterson's 2008 campaign were the American Farm Bureau, American Crystal Sugar, and the National Cattlemen's Beef Association. Overall, crop production, agricultural services/products, dairy, and food processing donated $628,687 to Peterson's campaign and political action committee, more than 41 percent of all the money he raised for the 2008 election. (Agriculture Committee members took in nearly $23 million in that election cycle alone from people and organizations with financial, insurance, and real estate affiliations, more than double what they received from anybody affiliated with actual agriculture.)

Like a manure pile at an Iowa factory pig farm, this stuff adds up. According to the Center for Public Integrity, the number of lobbyists devoted to climate change had risen by more than 400 percent since 2003 to a total of 2,810—giving lobbyists a five-to-one advantage over the combined membership of the House and Senate. (This is in contrast to an estimated 138 working on behalf of alternative forms of energy.) Targets for improving renewable energy resources were roughly halved as Congress gutted the EPA's authority to regulate carbon emissions. And rather than auction off pollution permits, as candidate Obama had proposed, the legislation offered 83 percent of them to polluters for free. All told, according to one analysis by Stanford University economists, polluters earned themselves $134 billion in taxpayer-funded gifts as they reduced the overall goal of a reduction in carbon emissions from 20 percent to 17 percent. Strongly supported by the financial industry, which stood to make billions on proposed carbon credit markets, this awful bill barely squeaked through the House by a 219 to 212 vote. Alas, it died there.

All this happened even though the evidence for human-made global warming continued to mount. In late July 2010, the U.S. National Atmospheric and Oceanic Administration (NOAA) issued its annual "State of the Climate" report, which confirmed that "the world is warming and the past decade was the warmest on record" and that NOAA's series of ten weather indicators "all tell the same story: Global warming is undeniable. . . . Glaciers and sea ice are melting, heavy rainfall is intensifying and heat waves are becoming more common and more intense." The influx of greenhouse gases into the atmosphere has hit oceans particularly hard, the NOAA report explained, as Arctic summer sea melting in 2010 is on track to be worse than 2007, when Arctic ice cover reached its lowest point on record. Even the U.S. military—a conservative institution if the word is to have any meaning whatever—noted in its 2010 Quadrennial Defense Review that climate change could "act as an accelerant of instability or conflict." Its authors were thinking about events such as the flood in the Indus Valley in Pakistan during the summer of 2010, which may have done more to destabilize that nation's pro-Western leadership than every al Qaida attack combined.

Environmental writer Bill McKibben notes that "the globally averaged temperature of the planet has been 57 degrees, give or take, for most of human history. . . . Now, the finest minds, using the finest equipment, tell us that it's headed toward 61 or 62 or 63 degrees." The result, according to the scientists of the National Aeronautics and Space Administration, is this new world will not be terribly "similar to that on which civilization developed and to which life on earth is adapted." What will it look like if no action is taken to curb carbon production? According to a report prepared by the

Guardian's Alok Jha for the 2009 Copenhagen climate change summit, we can expect the Amazon to turn into desert and grasslands, "while increasing CO_2 levels in the atmosphere make the world's oceans too acidic for remaining coral reefs and thousands of other marine life forms. More than 60 million people, mainly in Africa, would be exposed to higher rates of malaria. Agricultural yields around the world will drop and half a billion people will be at greater risk of starvation." That's in the near term. As the world's sea level begins to rise by twenty-three feet over the next few hundred years, one can expect glaciers to recede and thereby reduce the world's freshwater supply. As many as one-third of the world's species will likely become extinct as the 2°C rise changes their habitats too quickly for them to adapt.

With another degree of warming, Jha warns,

global warming may run out of control and efforts to mitigate it may be in vain. Millions of square kilometers of Amazon rainforest could burn down, releasing carbon from the wood, leaves and soil and thus making the warming even worse, perhaps by another 1.5 C. In southern Africa, Australia and the western US, deserts take over. Billions of people are forced to move from their traditional agricultural lands, in search of scarcer food and water. Around 30–50% less water is available in Africa and around the Mediterranean. In the UK, winter floods follow summers of droughts. Sea levels rise to engulf small islands and low-lying areas such as Florida, New York and London. The Gulf Stream, which warms the UK all year round, will decline and changes in weather patterns will lead to higher sea levels at the Atlantic coasts.

And, finally, should we stay on the path we're on, we can expect a 4° rise in the earth's average temperature. Jha explains:

At this stage, the Arctic permafrost enters the danger zone. The methane and carbon dioxide currently locked in the soils will be released into the atmosphere. At the Arctic itself, the ice cover would disappear permanently, meaning extinction for polar bears and other native species that rely on the presence of ice. Further melting of Antarctic ice sheets would mean a further 5m rise in the sea level, submerging many island nations. Italy, Spain, Greece and Turkey become deserts and mid-Europe reaches desert temperatures of almost 50C in summer. Southern England's summer climate could resemble that of modern southern Morocco.

McKibben argues that the 1,400-page collection of "offsets and sweeteners and bailouts . . . was an ugly deal—but nowhere near ugly enough for the Senate." (For instance, the bill as passed forbade the EPA from regulating carbon and prevented states from trying to implement tougher standards on their own.) He notes that an alternative bill, proposed by Maine Republican Susan Collins and Washington Democrat Maria Cantwell, sought to curb emissions by inviting energy companies to bid each year for their permits to put carbon in the atmosphere instead of merely giving them away. The money earned would be used "to write a check to every American every year." Gas prices would go up as the price of these permits was passed onto customers at the pump, but seven out of ten Americans would come out ahead in the end. (The only real losers would be the energy hogs among us.) "Cap and dividend" is a much simpler, easier, and more efficient way to regulate carbon emissions than cap and trade and much easier to sell to the average voter. So why isn't it being seriously considered? As physicist Joe Romm of Climate Progress told McKibben, "It's energy-intensive businesses that hate [cap and dividend], and I'm afraid they drive the process more than the public. If public support mattered, we'd have passed a bill a long time ago!"

To be fair to all concerned, climate change is a terribly complicated matter whose dangers remain, for most of us largely invisible, if not actually hypothetical. Representatives, like the rest of us, have meanwhile been barraged by misinformation about the issue, from oil companies and Glenn Beck and the local news meteorologist insisting that the science behind global warming is a big hoax designed in the service of Satan. Alleged scientific misconduct of the Climate Research Unit at the University of East Anglia—based on the selective revelation of stolen e-mails—allowed many in the media to write off the phenomenon for parts of 2009 and 2010 as this story was simultaneously misinterpreted and deliberately distorted by many media outlets that covered it. Careless, sensationalistic reporting played into the hands of those working to discredit the global scientific consensus behind the need to take urgent action to protect the planet. For instance, a 2002 memo by conservative political consultant Frank Luntz argued that if American "voters believe there is no consensus about global warming within the scientific community," political action to address the issue would remain stalled in Congress. Climate deniers therefore needed to embrace a tactic employed for decades by tobacco companies: Fund and publicize their own "studies" and research institutes. Historian Naomi Oreskes, coauthor of a book-length study of corporate manipulation of public opinion on science, notes, "If the answer is to phase out fossil fuels, a different group of people are going to be making money, so we shouldn't be surprised that they're fighting tooth and nail."

When in 2008 President Obama noted that the science underlying human-made global warming was "beyond dispute," the libertarian Cato Institute took out a full-page ad in the *New York Times* in an attempt to undermine what was then a statement of fact; the ad was just a warning shot in a campaign that has resonated with considerable success throughout the mainstream media. Ed Crane, the institute's founder and president, who enjoys no credentials whatever as a scientist, informed the *New Yorker*'s Jane Mayer that "global-warming theories" needed to be resisted because they "giv[e] the government more control of the economy." The Cato Institute was begun in 1977 with a grant from conservative billionaires Charles and David Koch. According to the Center for Public Integrity, between 1986 and 1993 the Koch family gave $11 million to the institute. These monies are just a small part of the nearly $200 million the brothers and their company gave away to such causes between 1998 and 2008—a figure that excludes the $50 million Koch Industries spent on lobbying and nearly $5 million more made in campaign contributions by its political action committee. (*Forbes* magazine calculates just Charles Koch's personal fortune at $21.5 billion.) As Mayer notes in her lengthy profile of the Kochs, Cato presently employs a hundred full-time workers, "and its experts and policy papers are widely quoted and respected by the mainstream media. It describes itself as nonpartisan, and its scholars have at times been critical of both parties. But it has consistently pushed for corporate tax cuts, reductions in social services, and laissez-faire environmental policies." The creation and sustenance of Cato, together with other right-wing think tanks such as the Heritage Foundation, the American Enterprise Institute, and the Hoover Institute at Stanford, have populated the media with a plethora of "scholars" whose arguments are allegedly based on "scientific facts gathered in the past 10 years [that] do not support the notion of catastrophic human-made warming."

The purposeful infection of the public dialogue on global warming with this virus of pseudoscience empowered conservatives to dismiss the entire scientific consensus as some sort of liberal conspiracy. To take just one of thousands of possibilities, an November 24, 2009, article in the conservative *Washington Times* bore the headline "Hiding Evidence of Global Cooling: Junk Science Exposed Among Climate-Change Believers." The article referred to the "baloney practices that pass as sound science about climate change." In the end, as Klaus

Hasselmann, emeritus director of the Max Planck Institute for Meteorology, reported in *Nature Geoscience* in August 2010, three separate investigations—"one by the UK House of Commons Science and Technology Committee, a second by the Scientific Assessment Panel of the Royal Society, chaired by Lord Oxburgh, and the latest by the Independent Climate Change E-mails Review, chaired by Sir Muir Russell—confirmed what climate scientists have never seriously doubted: established scientists, dependent on their credibility for their livelihood, have no motivation in purposely misleading the public and their colleagues." And yet thanks to climate deniers who exploited this story, as well as the inherent complexities of scientific research and prediction itself, in a March 2010 Gallup Poll nearly 50 percent of those questioned said that they believed the threat of global warming to be "generally exaggerated." This was a rise from 35 percent two years earlier. According to the same poll, a bare majority of 52 percent of Americans believed that "most scientists believe that global warming is occurring," down from 65 percent in 2008.

The results of this campaign have been profoundly heartening to these merchants of misinformation. When, for instance, Norman Dennison, a fifty-year-old Indiana electrician, told a reporter that global warming warnings constituted "a flat-out lie," basing his view on "the preaching of Rush Limbaugh and the teaching of Scripture," he was responding in part to the multiyear, multimillion-dollar campaign to discredit normative science by those who stand to profit from climate catastrophe. According to a study by the Center for American Progress Action Fund, just thirteen such right-wing groups spent more than $68.5 million in 2010 alone on "misleading and fictitious television ads designed to shape midterm elections and advance their anti-clean energy reform agenda." This was in addition to the nearly $500 million that Koch Industries and its allies in oil, coal, and utility businesses collectively had spent since the beginning of 2009 to lobby against legislation to address climate change and to defeat candidates who supported it. And guess what? According to a survey by *National Journal*, "Of the 20 Republican Senate candidates in contested races, 19 question the science of global warming and oppose any comprehensive legislation to deal with it."

FINANCIAL REGULATION

It's not difficult to see why sacrifices in the name of preventing the potential effects of climate change would be difficult for any politician to demand in this context. Even without deliberately deceptive debate and purposeful media know-nothingism, democracy simply does not work very well when costs are borne by the present but the payoff belongs to posterity. ("What has posterity ever done for me?" goes the old political cliché.) When one calculates the additional impact of the jobs crisis that faced Congress and the administration during this period, and the mountains of disinformation Americans received, it is easy to see why investing in climate control would be a particularly tough sell. But none of these conditions applied to the situation the Obama administration faced regarding financial regulation. Indeed, anger at Wall Street ran so high and continued for so long that it became a favorite theme for Republican candidates during the final weeks of the 2010 election. More than two hundred candidates around the country ran ads depicting their opponents as captives of an avaricious group of Wall Street bankers, with visuals including "Wall Street" street signs dissolving into scenes of cigar-smoking corporate fat cats swilling cocktails and laughing at how they had ripped off regular Americans. So when President Obama promised "I intend to hold these banks fully accountable" in his State of the Union address, his proposed reforms came with the added advantage of an enraged electorate and an unmistakable public mandate for strong action to prevent a repeat of 2008's emergency bailout.

But while considerable oratorical firepower was focused on AIG and Goldman Sachs in front of the TV cameras, in the back rooms of

Capitol Hill it was back to brandy and cigars. The banking industry has been making friends and influencing Congress for centuries. ("They frankly own the place," explained Senator Richard Durbin [D-IL] in 2009.)

Upon signing the financial regulation bill at a July 21 White House ceremony, President Obama pronounced, "These reforms represent the strongest consumer financial protections in history." And the bill did win some important victories for average people, particularly in the realm of credit card bills and other consumer-related protections. But on the really important issues of concern to the big banks with regard to both their investors and taxpayer liabilities, the compromises reached between House and Senate negotiators, following furious lobbying by almost everyone connected to the industry, looked very much like victories.

Back in January 2010 as the Obama administration's first anniversary was approaching, and as the details of the financial regulation legislation were still being negotiated in various congressional committees and subcommittees, an examination by the *Wall Street Journal* found that for all the ferocious rhetoric emanating from Washington about the indefensible behavior of so many spoiled and irresponsible members of the banking community, pretty much nothing of importance had changed in the way these same bankers went about their business. Back then the *Journal* explained:

> Credit-rating companies, excoriated for placing top grades on what turned out to be toxic debt, still face the same potential conflicts of interest they always faced: These companies are paid by the very parties churning out the debt that is being rated.
>
> Trading accounts for more than half the recent revenue of Wall Street firms, according to analysts. This suggests a continued dependence on volatile investment profits.

Just as important, there have been few big changes in markets for derivative securities, such as credit-default swaps.

Nor have rules been changed to increase the amount of
capital that U.S. banks must hold as a percentage of assets.

True, the bill did restrict some of the most egregious excesses of
the big banks' behavior—or at least appeared to do so. But when one
examined the fine print, there was far more smoke than actual fire.
For instance, in January 2009 a group of experts led by Paul Volcker,
a former Federal Reserve chair, a close economic adviser to President
Obama, and "the nation's senior financial authority" (John Cassidy
writing in the *New Yorker* in July 2010), issued a report for the Group
of Thirty, an organization of senior business executives and academ-
ics. The report declared, "Large, systemically important banking institutions should be restricted in undertaking proprietary activities that
represent particularly high risks and serious conflicts of interest." Yet
the legislation continued to abide by such trades on the banks' own
accounts in risky hedge funds and private equity funds. The limit on
these trades was originally intended, upon initial passage of the bill,
to be pegged at a generous 3 percent of any given bank's tangible equity. But thanks to a last-minute intervention on the part of the big
banks, this limit was redefined to apply to 3 percent of a bank's "Tier
1" capital, which, Matt Taibbi notes, is "a far bigger pool of money
that includes a bank's common shares and deferred-tax assets instead
of just preferred shares. In real terms, banks could now put up to 40
percent more into high-risk investments." Finally, insurers, mutual
funds, and trusts are completely exempt even from these extremely
generous limits.

A second last-minute change in the legislation helped to gut the
regulation that might have prevented banks from engaging in risky derivative trading—such as the credit-default swaps that almost crashed
the system—with the funds they received from unsuspecting deposi-

tors. The new law demands that trading now be separated out into bank subsidiaries created explicitly for this purpose. But most institutions managed to secure last-minute exemptions from the law, and those that did not need not worry themselves too much regarding enforcement. After passage, Goldman Sachs simply reclassified its proprietary traders—those who use the firm's own money—as asset managers and thereby made it just about impossible for anyone to distinguish between a trade made for a client and one made on the company's own behalf. "You can use client activity as a cover for basically anything you are doing," Janet Tavakoli, who runs her own structured finance consulting firm, told the *New York Times*.

In one of the most outrageous exploitations of the power of the lobbying process, auto companies were able to get Congress to exempt their finance arms from regulation by the new Consumer Financial Protection Bureau. This is not only illogical—these finance companies operate exactly as banks do—it is also awful public policy, as such companies are notorious for the abuses they generate under cover of car loans. (For most Americans, an automobile is the second-largest capital investment they make.) As legal scholar Lawrence Lessig observes, "When 'free-market' Republicans vote to support milk subsidies or sugar tariffs, or when 'pro-consumer' Democrats vote to exempt used-car dealers from consumer financial-protection legislation, it is easy to understand the mistrust and hard to believe that the influence of money hasn't weakened the ability of members to serve the principles, or even the interests, they were elected to represent."

The bill's creation of the new Consumer Protection Bureau must be counted as a victory. But the fact that it will be housed inside the bank-friendly Federal Reserve, rather than being a stand-alone agency, may prove a more-than-adequate consolation prize for the banks. And in yet another step toward even less regulation than occurred in precrisis conditions, the legislation will prevent the Securities and Exchange Commission (SEC) from regulating equity-indexed annuities, which have been a particular problem for elderly Americans who are confused by the fine print when sold these complicated financial instruments—often not by accident.

"Because of this law, the American people will never again be asked to foot the bill for Wall Street's mistakes," the president promised. "There will be no more taxpayer-funded bailouts. Period." But the truth is Obama was speaking more from hope than experience. In addition to the weaknesses already discussed—and more than a few that have yet to reveal themselves—Congress declined to curb the size of banks "too big to fail" and therefore to protect American taxpayers from being forced into future bailouts when these banks prove irresponsible once more. This means the big banks can still gamble with the house's money; they take home the winnings, but when their losses are large enough, it will be the taxpayer who foots the bill. These loans, no matter how risky, remain guaranteed by the Federal Reserve, the Treasury Department, and the Federal Deposit Insurance Corporation should they go sour. This problem, moreover, can only worsen, as the big American banks become increasingly global in their orientation and thereby put the entire world economic system at risk with their irresponsible investments, undertaken outside the authority of any U.S., or even West European, regulatory authority.

Executive pay, needless to say, also remained unlimited under the legislation, even for companies saved by the taxpayer-funded Troubled Asset Relief Program (TARP), unlike the European Community, which barely a month earlier had instituted strict compensation limits on its bankers. In 2008, the year of the big bailout, one trader alone—Andre Hall of the Phibro energy trading unit, which TARP participant Citigroup sold to Occidental Petroleum—went home with a bonus of $100 million. The next two years, 2009 and 2010, then turned out to be record years on Wall Street, as the three dozen top New York banks, investment banks, hedge funds, money-management firms, and securities exchanges prepared to pay out bonuses calculated by the *Wall Street Journal* at $139 billion and $144 billion, respectively. At the same time, these banks and quasi banks still received 0 percent (or near 0 percent) loans from the Fed, which provided the basis of its lending profits. No surprise, therefore, that the share prices of Citigroup, JP Morgan Chase, and Bank of America all rose on the morning of June 25 when the (near) final details of the deal were announced, despite drops across the board in most of the rest of the U.S. stock market. (This mirrored, by the way, the triple-digit rise in the stock market after the passage of the Obama health care bill despite countless pundit predictions, like that of CNBC's James Cramer, that the bill would "topple the stock market.")

"I do think that generally the banks should be pleased that it was not worse than it was," Jim Eckenrode, a banking analyst at TowerGroup, a financial services consulting firm, told the *New York Times* in what can only be considered one of the great understatements of 2010. And it's not only the banks that had reason to break out the champagne. Insurance companies also "mostly dodged" any significant federal oversight, as Jay MacDonald at Bankrate.com noted, even though AIG's egregiously careless behavior in the subprime mortgage market cost U.S. taxpayers between $150 and $200 billion. Nor did the legislation address the single most expensive part of the taxpayer bailout, which was the irresponsible behavior of Fannie Mae and Freddie Mac. They are free to continue just as before they ran up hundreds of billions of dollars in unsustainable loans—and, ultimately, taxpayer-guaranteed loans.

Unlike much of a starstruck media, industry insiders fully understood that the battle would continue long after the legislation had passed and most reporters had stopped paying attention. Owing to the complexity of the legislation, many, if not most, of the facts on the ground would be determined by fine print authored by regulatory

agencies. In the case of this bill, federal agencies were charged with
defining the final contours of at least 243 financial rules and charged
to conduct sixty-seven studies, according to an assessment by the
Davis Polk law firm. As Eric Lichtblau reports in the *New York Times*,
"The S.E.C. alone is responsible for developing 95 rules on topics like
the trading of derivatives, standards for credit rating agencies and disclosure of executive bonuses. The Commodity Futures Trading
Commission must develop 61 rules, the Federal Reserve has 54, and
two agencies just created by Congress—the Consumer Financial
Protection Bureau and the Financial Stability Oversight Council—
have 80 rules between them." Many of these will be written by former
and future members of the same firms being regulated and will naturally reflect those backgrounds and goals. Ezra Klein rightly observes,
it's a dynamic with "an incredibly moneyed and politically sophisticated industry massed on one side, and pretty much no one on the
other side." (According to CRP, 148 former regulatory officials were
registered to lobby the government in 2009 or 2010, representing virtually every regulatory agency.) Lichtblau adds, "Many directives in
the Congressional legislation are written so broadly that the agencies
have wide discretion in drafting rules," and within that context "credit
card companies will look to maintain higher fees on debit cards.
Derivatives investors will seek to define themselves as 'end users' of a
particular product who should be exempted from some restrictions.
Niche industries like payday lenders and check-cashing services will
push for less burdensome federal regulation. And in many cases, the
industries will rely on former regulators to make their cases to the federal agencies." How tough do you think these regulators are likely to
be when dealing with the most complicated technical aspects of the
new law and most members of the mainstream media have ceased to
pay attention?

  In the meantime, some of these companies will employ their
strategic and political muscle to simply refuse to cooperate with the

new legislation at all. For instance, rather than submit to the strictures demanding honest assessment of risk lest they be faced with financial penalties, Wall Street's credit ratings agencies—the very ones that had blessed so many worthless credit-default swaps and other ultimately worthless real estate deals—effectively went on strike and refused to allow bond issuers to use their ratings. As a result, the *Wall Street Journal* reported, "the $1.4 trillion market for autos, student loans and credit cards—things came to a halt." When both Ben Bernanke and Rush Limbaugh, among others, came to the aid of the agencies in public debate, the Securities and Exchange Commission suspended the new law for six months, for starters. What's more, the fine print of the new legislation gave the SEC a privacy mandate similar to what bank regulators enjoy exempting them, according to Reuters, "from having to turn over to the media information it gathers from financial institutions in its expanded supervisory role." Overall, as William K. Black, a professor of economics and law at the University of Missouri, Kansas City, notes,

> the fundamental problem with the financial reform bill is that it would not have prevented the current crisis and it will not prevent future crises because it does not address the reason the world is suffering recurrent, intensifying crises. A witches' brew of deregulation, desupervision, regulatory black holes and perverse executive and professional compensation has created an intensely criminogenic environment that produces epidemics of accounting control fraud that hyper-inflate financial bubbles and cause economic crises. The bill continues the unlawful, unprincipled and dangerous policy of allowing systemically dangerous institutions (SDIs) to play by special rules even when they are insolvent. Indeed, the bill makes a variety of accounting control fraud lawful.

THE POWER OF CULTURE

The bankers' success had many sources, of course. There is much more to the money culture in Congress than ever appears on a contribution list; indeed, Washington operates on a culture of implied bribery no less than it does the real thing. According to Public Citizen, more than seventy ex-members of Congress could be found lobbying for Wall Street and the financial services sector in 2009, including two former Senate majority leaders (Trent Lott and Bob Dole), two former House majority leaders (Richard Gephardt and Dick Armey), and a former House speaker (Dennis Hastert). At the staff level, the numbers are even more impressive. When Representative Barney Frank (D-MA) publicly rebuked his former aide Peter S. Roberson in April 2010 for switching sides to Goldman Sachs immediately after helping to draft the derivative regulations likely to affect his new employer, the chair of the House Financial Services Committee treated the occurrence as a relatively rare one. It was not. In fact, as a lengthy Huffington Post investigation revealed in December 2009, it happens almost every day. Two hundred forty-three people have worked on the House Banking Committee staff since 2000, and 126 of them have left the committee. Of these, 62 have registered as lobbyists, largely in the financial industry, while others lobby at law firms and such without being required to fill out forms. Given that the 243 figure includes clerical and technological staff, this means that almost everyone with any expertise on the committee has gone off to sell it to the people whose work they are professing to regulate.

This particular gravy train travels in both directions. Former clients of current committee staff members include H&R Block, the New York Stock Exchange, the Bond Market Association, Wachovia, MetLife, and Experian. Not a one has any experience lobbying for consumer organizations such as the Consumer Federation of America, Public Citizen, USPIRG, or, God forbid, ACORN. And this practice is hardly limited to bank lobbyists. At the time of the BP oil spill, more than 400 of the industry's 600 registered lobbyists were former government employees, including 18 ex-members of Congress and dozens of former presidential appointees.

This is just the way it is. No stigma is attached. No eyebrows are raised when a staffer "moves downtown." Rather, it is "a very logical progression," according to retired committee lawyer Howard Menell. The implied transaction can be seen in the carefully coded discussions that take place at the endless stream of receptions, seminars (really, sponsored vacations), and happy hours offered by these same trade organizations, whose representatives are always happy to lend their expertise to the often-harried staffer. In fact, lobbyists need not apologize for the role they play in shaping public policy for private gain in Washington according to its current cultural mores. They are celebrated for it. If you doubt this, check out the daily "Playbook," published every morning by Mike Allen of *Politico*, the new bible of political self-promotion in the form of a tipsheet of what's on for the day. Reports of social gatherings, hirings, birthdays, and weddings of lobbyists occupy the same space with the same importance as those of senators and editors in chief. When the publication threw a lavishly catered 2010 election party at the Newseum in Washington, one reporter who attended noted that "weirdly, no one was reacting to any of the calls any of the muted TV anchors made. Probably because to the lobbyists and defense contractors who made up the bulk of the crowd, little was actually going to change; they might have an easier time getting some requests filled, but mostly, a shift in power just means a shift in which offices you need to visit to get legislative favors."

Rather than being perceived as pimps or prostitutes, corporate lobbyists are beloved members of the new political establishment where everybody does everybody else's jobs and no hard and fast lines can be found anywhere—save those between winning and losing. After all, government pay does not even begin to approach the levels earned on

Wall Street or inside the nation's top law firms. Salaries being what they are, aside from proximity to power, the key perk in Washington is the ability to live beyond one's means. Journalists, with few exceptions, have lost what were once generous expense accounts and can no longer pick up three- and four-figure dinner checks as a matter of course. Staffers never could. The only people left with cash to make life worth living luxury-wise are the lobbyists, and none are richer than bank lobbyists, whose earnings and bonuses are twice the average elsewhere in the private economy, much less in the public sector. During the first eighteen months of the Obama presidency, then-House Minority Leader John Boehner, funneling money through his political action committee, the Freedom Project, enjoyed trips costing more than $67,000 at the Ritz-Carlton Naples in Florida; at least $20,000 at the Robert Trent Jones Golf Club in Gainesville, Virginia; and more than $29,000 at the Muirfield Village Golf Club in Dublin, Ohio, according to federal records examined by the *New York Times*. Between 2000 to 2007, he and his wife enjoyed no fewer than forty-five flights on private corporate jets in addition to $340,000 in contributions from just one industry: tobacco. And as the 2010 congressional session came to an end, Republican staffers were reported to be entertaining offers of around $1 million a year to move "downtown" and work for "K Street" lobbyists. "We're seeing a premium for Republicans," explains Ivan H. Adler, who headhunts lobbyists for Washington's McCormick Group. "They're the new 'It' girl." In the fall of 2010, a study published by the London School of Economics found that when a U.S. senator left office, ex-staffers-turned-lobbyists earned 24 percent less money for their firms. In real dollar amounts that equaled $177,000 of the $744,000 of their estimated annual worth. "The next year?" joshed retiring Senate Banking Committee Finance chair Chris Dodd, twenty of whose staffers had already moved to K Street. "I better tell that to my staff. . . . Don't go to K Street." In fact, the Center for Public Integrity's reports reveal that in Obama's Washington there are actually fewer lobbyists than before, but they spend more money. If nothing else, Obama has succeeded in raising the price of buying what you want in Congress.

Lobbyists for the banking industry benefit immensely from the favors they can offer and the jobs they may dangle but also from their success in creating and propagating an entire ideological framework that does their work for them for free among members of Congress and the media. In his famous prison notebooks, discovered long after his death, Italian communist philosopher Antonio Gramsci identified, in the words of one of his interpreters, "an order in which a certain way of life and thought is dominant, in which one concept of reality is infused throughout society in all its institutional and private manifestations, informing with its spirit all taste, morality, customs, religious and political principles, and all social relations, particularly in their intellectual and moral connotations." Economists Simon Johnson and James Kwak identify just such an "order" in the United States beginning in the 1990s, when both parties benefited from massive investments in congressional war chests by investment bankers and their allies to build on the belief of what Ronald Reagan liked to call the "magic" of the marketplace. The new ideology of Wall Street they identify, "that unfettered innovation and unregulated financial markets were good for America and the world," soon became the consensus view in both the Democratic and Republican parties. As a result, lobbyists' talking points became "self-evident."

This ideology had three components. First was the "idea that financial innovation, like technological innovation, was necessarily good." Second was the idea that complex financial transactions served the noble purpose of helping ordinary Americans buy houses. Third was the notion that Wall Street was the most exciting place to be at the turn of the new millennium. Johnson and Kwak note that Alan Greenspan—now repentant, but for a long time perhaps the most admired man in all Washington, as well as being a longtime acolyte of radical libertarian novelist (and for some, guru), Ayn Rand—was the pied piper of the ideology of finance. Speaking to the annual conference of something called the Association of Private Enterprise Education, the oracle decreed:

> With technological change clearly accelerating, existing regulatory structures are being bypassed, freeing market forces to enhance wealth creation and economic growth. . . . As we move into a new century, the market-stabilizing private regulatory forces should gradually displace many cumbersome, increasingly ineffective government structures. This is a likely outcome since governments, by their nature, cannot adjust sufficiently quickly to a changing environment, which too often veers in unforeseen directions. The current adult generations are having difficulty adjusting to the acceleration of the uncertainties of today's silicon driven environment. Fortunately, our children appear to thrive on it. The future accordingly looks bright.

Consider for a moment the power of an ideology that accomplishes the following: During one week in the autumn of 2010, the U.S. Census Bureau reported that the number of Americans living in poverty had reached its highest level in fifteen years. (For a single adult in 2009, the poverty line was $10,830 in pretax cash income. For a family of four, it was $22,050.) So, too, did economic inequality. A few days after the census report, *Forbes* magazine released its annual list of the four hundred richest Americans and their combined net worth, which had climbed 8 percent to $1.37 trillion. Another report, this one from the Corporation for Enterprise Development and the Annie E. Casey Foundation, found that the U.S. government had spent nearly $400 billion during fiscal year 2009 to fund tax breaks and programs aimed at helping Americans build wealth. More than half the benefits in question went to the wealthiest 5 percent of tax-payers, individuals and households making more than $167,000. The top 1 percent of taxpayers, those making more than $1 million, re-ceived an average of $95,000 in assistance. Meanwhile, families mak-ing $50,000 received less than $500 in benefits.

So what was the crucial economic debate taking place in Congress as these reports were released and unemployment continued to hover at 10 percent (conservatively defined) and politicians of both parties bemoaned the exploding federal deficit? Naturally, it was a fight over whether to make permanent the Bush tax cuts aimed exclusively at in-dividuals earning $250,000 a year or more at an estimated cost, ac-cording to Congressional Budget Office figures, of $4 trillion. Even the Democrats refused to debate the issue, fearing that the willingness to tax the wealthiest Americans would somehow cast them as "class warriors" in a debate exclusively dominated by the demands of the superrich.

Together with the money and the revolving jobs door, and the cul-tural capital Wall Street enjoyed as the home of what Tom Wolfe calls "Masters of the Universe," Johnson and Kwak note, "these powerful forces [give] Wall Street a degree of political influence that no amount of payoffs to corrupt politicians could have bought." Don Lucchese, Michael Corleone's rival for control of the vast riches of the mafia's worldwide finances, sums this philosophy up pretty well in the much underrated *The Godfather, Part III*: "Finance is a gun," he explains to Vincent, Michael's nephew. "Politics is knowing when to pull the trigger.

"CRAZY, ANTI-BUSINESS LIBERALS"

New York Democratic senator Charles Schumer operates on a similar set of principles. Even though he portrays himself as a populist fighter for the middle class, this putatively liberal senator from one of America's most liberal states nevertheless does the bidding for Wall Street to an impressive degree and does so with great effectiveness, given his position as both a member of the Banking and Finance Committees and vice chair of the party conference, as well as a former chair of the Democratic Senatorial Campaign Committee, in which capacity he raised some $240 million, much of it from the financial industries. Speaking to an industry breakfast in the days when all seemed sunny on Wall Street, this putative populist promised, "We are not going to be a bunch of crazy, anti-business liberals. . . . We are going to be effective, moderate advocates for sound economic policies, good responsible stewards you can trust." Reporting in the *New York Times*, Eric Lipton and Raymond Hernandez note that New York's senior senator "embraced the industry's free market, deregulatory agenda more than almost any other Democrat in Congress, even backing some measures now blamed for contributing to the financial crisis. . . . He succeeded in limiting efforts to regulate credit-rating agencies, for example, sponsored legislation that cut fees paid by Wall Street firms to finance government oversight, pushed to allow banks to have lower capital reserves and called for the revision of regulations to make corporations' balance sheets more transparent."

Schumer also played a powerful role during the financial regulation negotiations when he rallied to protect banks' right to gamble with their investors' funds. And much earlier than that he eagerly worked to protect the outsized paydays of hedge fund managers from normal taxation rules and thereby allow them to get away with paying taxes on just a fraction of their earnings compared to the rest of us. I got a chance to ask him about this once, though significantly, it happened at a $1,000 per person fund-raiser for Hillary Clinton's presidential campaign at the almost impossibly expansive Hamptons estate of Wall Street titan Ron Perlman. (I did not pay, alas.) Was it fair, I asked my senator, that our host paid a far smaller portion of his earnings in taxes than did the waiters and waitresses serving us the stuffed canapés? Schumer, clearly annoyed, told me that he thought it was fair to tax hedge fund billionaires at the normal rate only if we did other partnerships, like lawyers. In other words, it was a question of fairness only to the wealthy. Working stiffs like the wait staff around us did not even enter into his calculation.

John C. Bogle, founder and former chairman of the Vanguard Group, considers Schumer to be "serving the parochial interest of a very small group of financial people, bankers, investment bankers, fund managers, private equity firms, rather than serving the general public" and thereby "hurt[ing] the American investor first and the average American taxpayer." And, remember, Schumer is considered by many in the mainstream media to be "a big government liberal" (though Schumer ranks himself only about the twentieth most liberal member of the body). Imagine if some brave soul in a position of power akin to Schumer's had tried to represent the interests of the wait staff at Ron Perlman's house. What names might he have been called? Remember, your (shrinking) newspaper does not have a labor section. It does not have an environment section. And it most certainly does not have a human rights section. But it sure has a business section, just as your cable stations and radio dial are filled to the proverbial brim with programming devoted exclusively to news of interest to business but none at all to workers, much less the unemployed, the underemployed, or even those without sufficient disposable income to play the market.

MONEY, TALKING

The problems caused by money in our political system are certain to worsen in the near future as a result of a recent series of Supreme Court rulings that vastly expanded the rights of corporations and wealthy individuals to employ their riches to influence elections as they simultaneously weakened the strictures of accountability that had previously applied in such cases. In the early summer of 2010, an administration-backed bill called the Disclose Act—designed to force corporations and other donors who participate in political activity to disclose their top five donors and to agree to other disclosures in connection with expenditures prior to elections—had already been rewritten to exempt the eight-hundred-pound gorilla of political intimidation, the National Rifle Association. But the bill still foundered as all the other interests that cherished the notion of secrecy found legislators to do their bidding. (A September 2010 vote on the bill was coincidentally scheduled for the day *after* a $2,500 to $15,200 per place fund-raising dinner for the Democratic Senate Campaign Committee and the Democratic Congressional Campaign Committee.) Next, in late August, when few were paying attention, the Federal Election Commission (FEC)—led by its three Republican-appointed members—released a rather obscure report, called a "Statement of Reasons," indicating that it would interpret the new disclosure requirements in the most narrow fashion possible. This functioned as an engraved invitation to global corporations and wealthy individuals to exploit any number of easily imaginable loopholes to avoid even the most rudimentary reporting regulations.

These rulings have opened up new opportunities for all funders, but none so much as those working through the U.S. Chamber of Commerce, which functions as a kind of "fence" for many corporations looking to intervene in the political process without leaving any footprints. Grover Norquist, who acts as a combination of overseer, middleman, and occasional *capo di tutti capi* of the myriad right-wing lobbies that dot the Beltway, notes that, even though the Chamber of Commerce is not the most reliable of ideological allies, it is one of the most welcome. "K Street is a three-billion-dollar weathervane," Norquist told the *New Yorker*. "When Obama was strong, the Chamber of Commerce said, 'We can work with the Obama Administration.' But that changed when thousands of people went into the street and 'terrorized' congressmen. . . . Now that Obama is weak, people are getting tough."

The chamber has gone into business procuring advertisements that target candidates without revealing who is paying for the ads. In

August 2010, as the Associated Press reported, "the country's largest business lobby has pledged to spend $75 million in this year's elections. That's on top of a lobbying effort that already has cost the organization nearly $190 million since Barack Obama became president in January 2009." According to FEC filings, 96 percent of the chamber's spending during Obama's presidency as of September 2010 was dispensed in the service of Republican candidates. Among the donations revealed by a lengthy *New York Times* investigation of individual corporations' tax filings were the following:

- $2 million from Prudential Financial to fight financial regulation
- $1.7 million from Dow Chemical to weaken tighter security requirements on chemical facilities
- $8 million from Goldman Sachs, Chevron, Texaco, and Aegon, a multinational insurance company based in the Netherlands, to a chamber foundation critical of growing federal regulation and spending

According to John Motley, a former lobbyist for the National Federation of Independent Business, the chamber's pitches to corporate leaders in the hopes of transforming Congress have "changed the game" in Washington. "They've raised it to a science, and an art form."

The chamber is just one of many organizations jumping into this new business. Former Bush political guru Karl Rove began an organization, Crossroads Grassroots Policy Strategies/American Crossroads, that raised $50 million in contributions in just a few months in mid-2010, with estimates of its ultimate haul running as high as $250 million and little likelihood of much scrutiny of its donor lists. (One incomplete list filed with the FEC indicated that during the month of August 91 percent of the donations came from just three billionaire donors. In September Texas homebuilder Bob Perry gave $7 million alone, or nearly half of the $15 million that came in that month.) Sharing office space with Rove's Crossroads organizations is the American Action Network, founded by Republican operative Fred Malek, who first came to public attention with the release of Richard Nixon's Watergate tapes, on which, as White House personnel chief, he was heard dutifully accepting his president's directive to tally up the number of Jews serving in the Department of Labor as the president suspected them of disloyalty. Malek was later identified by the *Washington Post* as the driving force behind Nixon's "responsiveness program," which intended to "politicize the federal government in support of Nixon's reelection." His organization undertook a $19 million ad campaign in 2010 designed to defeat Democrats in twenty-two House districts with a series of misleading claims and deliberate disinformation. The network refuses, however, to identify its funders.

A snapshot of the overall effect of such spending could be found one week in September when, apparently typically, Republicans candidates outspent Democrats by a seven-to-one margin in Senate races and a four-to-one margin in House contests.

This avalanche of cash was just the tip of the new, uncontrolled corporate spending iceberg emerging from a series of Supreme Court decisions. In the most important of these, 2009's *Citizens United v. Federal Election Commission*, the one-vote conservative majority somehow concluded "that independent expenditures, including those made by corporations, do not give rise to corruption or the appearance of corruption. That speakers may have influence over or access to elected officials does not mean that those officials are corrupt. And the appearance of influence or access will not cause the electorate to lose faith in this democracy." Significantly, the Court did even not distinguish between monies spent by American citizens to influence our elections and those contributed by foreign donors. The justices said they preferred to address the "question [of] whether the Government has a compelling interest in preventing foreign individuals or associations from influencing our Nation's political process" in another case on another day.

These amazing arguments earned corporations a right that wealthy individuals have enjoyed since 1976's *Buckley v. Valeo*: the right to spend an unlimited amount on independent campaign expenditures. And spend they did. Conservative groups came to view the new ruling as a kind of "Good Housekeeping seal of approval," according to one right-wing fund-raiser, and a "psychological green light," according to another. A study published on the Web site Think Progress calculated that by August 2010 various conservative groups had already pledged to spend roughly $400 million in so-called independent expenditures for the coming November elections, all of it going to Republicans. Even if we allow for a bit of braggadocio, these numbers dwarfed what had been spent in previous midterm elections, more than doubling the amount spent four years earlier. And even though it may be true, as the noted philosopher Cyndi Lauper has observed that "money changes everything," money merely reinforces other factors in the larger culture. Americans are often said to be philosophically liberal but programmatically conservative. Such tendencies are reinforced by what appears to be a historically immutable libertarian streak, coupled with a distrust of centralized power in both liberal and conservative political traditions, both of which considerably complicate any efforts at liberal reform.

It was liberal hero Thomas Paine who first called government "but a necessary evil" and Henry David Thoreau who, writing in support of civil disobedience, observed that "the government is best which governs least." Both sentiments retain a powerful appeal to many Americans regardless of the merits of any given government program. When more than two centuries later Texas governor Rick Perry tells his fellow Republicans that the party should search out candidates who promise to "go to Washington, DC, and try to make it as inconsequential in your life as you can make it," he is giving voice to a longtime American predisposition popular across parties and ideologies. An April 2010 poll published by the Pew Research Center found that just 22 percent of the Americans questioned trusted the "government in Washington almost always or most of the time," one of the lowest levels in half a century.

This natural skepticism toward government action has been reinforced during this same period by a massive ideological investment by conservative individuals and foundations—aided by global corporations—in discrediting activist government and presenting the ideological doctrine of laissez-faire economics as the natural order of life. Lewis Powell laid out the ambitions of wealthy conservatives in a now infamous 1971 memo to the director of the U.S. Chamber of Commerce: to use their financial power to transform American political culture into one in which wealth and power could be unleashed upon the rest of us without the need for stealth or even explanation. Powell, who was later appointed by Richard Nixon to the U.S. Supreme Court, identified the enemy not as the remnants of the late-1960s antiwar and civil rights movements, both of which were in the process of disintegration and self-immolation. Rather, this "New Right" sought to undermine the "respectable elements of society," whom he intended to replace with people like themselves.

Neoconservative pundit Irving Kristol, *Wall Street Journal* editorial page editor Robert Bartley, and former Secretary of the Treasury William Simon, among others, made the cause of this new conservative culture a crusade throughout much of the 1970s and 1980s, with impressive, often astonishing results. They helped channel hundreds of millions of dollars, later mushrooming into billions, into the newly created conservative counterestablishment. And the sums were astonishing. The Koch Family Foundation alone ponied up $30 million dollars to promote its views via contributions to George Mason University, in Arlington, Virginia, and its Mercatus Center, which proudly proclaims itself to be "the world's premier university source for market-oriented ideas—bridging the gap between academic ideas and real-world problems." And it was just one of many.

These groups and others championed the arguments of Austrian economist Friedrich von Hayek and his American counterpart, monetarist Milton Friedman, to replace what had previously been a global Keynesian consensus with their own. These ideas were further disseminated by a rash of new quasi-academic and political journals and publishing houses, later augmented by an entire alternative media structure we now understand to be a natural part of our political and cultural landscape. One effect of this investment, evident since the Carter administration, has been a rush toward deregulation in virtually all areas of the economy under presidents of both parties. Lower taxes, less regulation, less government: These are seen as goals in and of themselves, regardless of their impact on public policy, because they weaken government's ability to intervene in the lives of its citizens. Milton Friedman argued that "freedom in economic arrangements is itself a component of freedom broadly understood, so economic freedom is an end in itself." This belief leads a conservative columnist like George F. Will to support policies such as the privatization of Social Security purely on ideological grounds—"reasons [that] rise from the philosophy of freedom"—and irrespective of issues of efficacy or equity. It was in this period, as intellectual historian Daniel T. Rodgers explains, that the "near global dominance of the new political economy" became evident. "Faith in the wisdom and the efficiency of markets, disdain for big government taxation, spending and regulation, reverence for a globalized world of flexible labor pools, free trade and free-floating capital" became the dominant ideology of American politics. The behavior of financial markets became a kind of substitute for democracy. As Citibank's Walter Wriston puts it, "Markets are voting machines. They function by taking referenda."

As late as November 2010, in the midst of America's most extensive economic downturn since the Great Depression, these referenda remained firmly in the conservative camp. While liberals across America were lamenting the Obama administration's failure to inject sufficient stimulus into the economy to revive consumer spending and commercial investment—and with them, its own political fortunes— no less influential a figure than Federal Reserve Chair Ben Bernanke felt compelled to assert to a gathering of the top members of his profession, "I grasp the mantle of Milton Friedman. . . . I think we are doing everything Milton Friedman would have us do."

Indeed, the entire edifice of supply-side economics was constructed and promoted with this goal in mind. It was Irving Kristol's neoconservative public policy journal, *Public Interest*, that gave supply-side economics its only favorable hearing in any kind of remotely respectable academic journal before Ronald Reagan embraced it in the presidential campaign of 1980. In 1995 Kristol admitted that he "was not certain of [the doctrine's] economic merits but quickly saw its political possibilities." What were these? To attack the "fundamental assumptions of contemporary liberalism that were my enemy. . . . Political effectiveness was the priority." Writing in 2010, *Financial Times* columnist Martin Wolf notes what he calls the "political genius of this idea," adding:

> Supply-side economics transformed Republicans from a minority party into a majority party. It allowed them to promise lower taxes, lower deficits and, in effect, unchanged spending. Why should people not like this combination? Who does not like a free lunch? How did supply-side economics bring these benefits? First, it allowed conservatives to ignore deficits. They could argue that, whatever the impact of the tax cuts in the short run, they would bring the budget back into balance, in the longer run. Second, the theory gave an economic justification—the argument from incentives—for lowering taxes on politically important supporters. Finally, if deficits did not, in fact, disappear,

conservatives could fall back on the "starve the beast" theory: deficits would create a fiscal crisis that would force the government to cut spending and even destroy the hated welfare state. In this way, the Republicans were transformed from a balanced-budget party to a tax-cutting party. This innovative stance proved highly politically effective, consistently putting the Democrats at a political disadvantage.

Conservative ideologues have simultaneously launched a rearguard action to recast previous progressive and liberal politicals as failures and, when possible, to remove them from historical accounts entirely. An extreme example of this is the victory of the fundamentalist Christian majority on the Texas school board in rewriting American history in order to downgrade the importance of virtually every non-right-wing individual or social movement that has ever had any impact on American life, including, most particularly, union organizers, immigrant workers, liberal legislators such as Ted Kennedy, and, believe it or not, the philosophy of the Enlightenment. (Proponents of separation of church and state throughout American history—surprise, surprise—did not fare well in the revised versions of Texas textbooks.)

The results of this deliberate dumbing-down of children in Texas and elsewhere will not be visible for years, but it is not difficult to see the results of the right-wing campaign throughout our political discourse. Over and over during the raucous health care town hall meetings in the summer of 2009, which were credited by Grover Norquist with exciting the Chamber of Commerce to take on Obama, citizens would stand up and scream some variant of "Keep your government hands off my Medicare." At one such meeting Representative Robert Inglis (R-SC) noted, "I had to politely explain that, 'Actually, sir, your healthcare is being provided by the government.' . . . But he wasn't having any of it." In some cases, citizens are genuinely ignorant regarding these issues. Americans are, after all, no strangers to deeply held beliefs based on misinformation. But frequently this confusion is the direct product of cynical manipulation by conservative elites, such as Norquist and his funders, which have somehow managed to help spark a movement of ordinary people going to the barricades to fight for the well-being of the funders of Norquist's many organizations.

THE BUYING OF "INDIANS"

The combination of these factors presents a problem for much of Obama's agenda because corporate America and its apologists in the media are always eager to portray almost any government program— or even necessary regulation—as the first step on the road to serfdom. Marc Morano, an ex-Senate staffer who now runs the conservative Climate Depot, warned his fellow citizens that if Obama's mild cap-and-trade plan was implemented, "the government is going to monitor where you set your thermostat, how much plane travel you do. . . . It's a level of control we've never even contemplated in America." So long as one is not too concerned by the veracity of one's statements, this logic can be applied to almost anything.

In the age of Obama, right-wing billionaires and corporate titans have also succeeded on another front, one that allows them to put a populist gloss on their unchanging agenda. In doing so, they appear to have solved what conservative scholar Bruce Bartlett describes as the right-wing libertarians' age-old problem of being "all chiefs and no Indians." And when Bartlett says "no," he means no. Back in 1980 when oil billionaire David C. Koch ran for vice president on the Libertarian Party ticket, his platform endorsed the abolition of Social Security, federal regulatory agencies, the FBI, the CIA, public schools, and just about anything else, as Jane Mayer observes, that "either inhibit[ed] his business profits or increase[d] his taxes." He polled barely 1 percent of the popular vote. Today Koch not only funds a vast network of pseudo-scientific organizations to undermine legitimate climate science, as discussed earlier; he also funds Tea Party groups that provide foot soldiers to march on behalf of his, and his fellow pluto-crats', financial and political interests. For instance, the Americans for Prosperity Foundation, which gave its Blogger of the Year Award to somebody who termed Barack Obama America's "cokehead in chief" and accused him of "demonic possession," was founded by David Koch, who remains its chairman. This foundation received more than $5 mil-lion from Koch foundations in 2005–2008 alone. The group's literature complains—rather ironically given the source of its funding—that "today, the voices of average Americans are being drowned out by lobby-ists and special interests. . . . But you can do something about it." The group helps to train Tea Party organizers and fund their demonstrations, often working in tandem with Dick Armey's FreedomWorks (formerly, Citizens for a Sound Economy), also funded by the Kochs to the tune of $12 million. Speaker after speaker at these events complain of what they call the Obama administration's "socialist vision for this country." As one Republican consultant explains, "The Koch brothers gave the money that founded it. It's like they put the seeds in the ground. Then the rain-storm comes, and the frogs come out of the mud—and they're our candidates!"

The Koch brothers sit atop a pyramid of funders, both individual and corporate, that have spent the past half-century seeking to reshape American politics to their liking. Groups with anodyne-sounding names, such as American Future Fund (AFF), are really little more than tools of wealthy industrialists. The AFF, a conservative organiza-tion based in Iowa, though its only headquarters is a rented UPS mail-box, proclaims a mission to provide "Americans with a conservative and free market viewpoint." The AFF receives significant funding— just how much is impossible to discern—from Bruce Rastetter, a co-founder and the chief executive of one of the nation's biggest ethanol companies, Hawkeye Energy Holdings. During the 2010 election cy-cle the AFF proudly took credit for launching "TV Ads in 13 States Targeting Liberal Politicians" all across the country, costing someone millions of dollars. And lo and behold, in addition to its electioneering, the *New York Times* reports, the AFF's "activities also seemed to dovetail with the interests of the ethanol industry." It even ran radio ads attacking a local racing association that was planning to power its cars with sugar-based ethanol from Brazil rather than from U.S. producers, as if this were somehow inconsistent with the fund's commitment to an unfettered "free market viewpoint."

And the all chiefs, no Indians nature of these organizations has no bearing on their electoral effectiveness. The Concerned Taxpayers of America (CTA) worked tirelessly to defeat Democratic congressional candidates in Maryland. It turned out to represent exactly two taxpayers. But give the CTA credit. Its membership is double that of Taxpayers Against Earmarks, which describes itself as "dedicated to educating and engaging American taxpayers about wasteful government spending and the misguided practice of earmarks" and poured millions into races in support of conservative Republicans across the country. Alas, the "taxpayers" were really just one taxpayer, Joe Ricketts, founder of Ameritrade and owner of the Chicago Cubs, who voluntarily disclosed his identity, though he was not required to do so by law. Nevertheless, money is money.

Yet voters are rarely, if ever, informed about who is behind these angry ads. What one Obama adviser calls this "grassroots citizens' movement brought to you by a bunch of oil billionaires" is quite a racket, almost comical in its underlying hypocrisy, and yet owing to a variety of weaknesses both in the political system generally and in the media particularly, it is able to successfully manipulate our system on behalf of the monied interests whose funds determine its direction.

CHAPTER FIVE

I Read the News Today, Oh Boy

A key reason the problems with our system go largely undiscussed in the mainstream media is that they are, to a significant degree, mirrored there. Back in the spring of 1969, journalist Pete Hamill prophetically described the as-yet-undiagnosed "Revolt of the White Lower Middle Class," together with its relation to what he called "the information explosion." Speaking of the white, largely ethnic denizens of the working-class boroughs of Queens, Brooklyn, and Staten Island, he wrote:

> Television has made an enormous impact on them, and because of the nature of that medium—its preference for the politics of theatre, its seeming inability to ever explain what is happening behind the photographed image—much of their understanding of what happens is superficial. Most of them have only a passing acquaintance with blacks, and very few have any black friends. So they see blacks in terms of militants with Afros and shades, or crushed people on welfare. . . . And in the past five or six years, with urban rioting on everyone's minds, they have provided themselves (or been provided with) a confused, threatening stereotype of blacks that has made it almost impossible to suggest any sort of black-white working-class coalition. . . . The working-class white man is actually in

revolt against taxes, joyless work, the double standards and short memories of professional politicians, hypocrisy and what he considers the debasement of the American dream. [But if] the stereotyped black man is becoming the working-class white man's enemy, the eventual enemy might be the democratic process itself.

The phenomenon discerned by Hamill more than forty years ago has exploded like a mushroom cloud in today's media environment, with consequences very much like those he predicted. Fox News is by far America's most popular cable news network, and its lead over MSNBC and CNN just keeps growing. In prime time, Fox hosts regularly attract more viewers than both competitors combined. (During the prime-time hours of Election Day 2010, for instance, Fox nearly doubled the viewership of the other two stations combined, with an average of nearly 7 million viewers compared to just 2.4 million for CNN and fewer than 2 million for MSNBC.) This is a matter of considerable political significance for the potential success of any progressive president because the number one cable news network in America just happens to be dedicated to a program of purposeful misinformation rather than any honest accounting of the news—"a cyclonic, perpetual emotion machine that gins up legitimate political disagreements into a full-fledged panic attack about the next coming of Chairman Mao," as Jon Stewart told Bill O'Reilly during one of his periodic visits to O'Reilly's show.

The Fox News channel is often described as a cable news station. On occasion, the word "conservative" or "biased" is attached to that description. But few dispute the journalistic orientation of the overall enterprise. This is a mistake. Fox is something new—something for which we do not yet have a word. It provides almost no actual journalism. Instead, it gives ideological guidance to the Republican Party and millions of its supporters, attacking its opponents and keeping its supporters in line. And because Fox manages to earn over a half a billion dollars a year, according to 2009 figures, in doing so, it functions as the equivalent of a political perpetual motion machine.

Fox's broadcasting is deeply biased against liberals in almost every way imaginable. Fox News broadcasters regularly distort what the president says or cut away before letting him finish. They invite Republican politicians and conservative propagandists to come on and lie outright about both people and policy and then build on those lies to tell even larger lies. They invite faux liberals to come on the air to attack the real thing. In doing so, they engage in conspiracy theories so lurid and outlandish that one is tempted to turn on old episodes of *The Twilight Zone* for a reality check. They all but ignore Republican scandals and obsess about Democratic ones.

WHO'S ZOOMING WHOM?

"Republicans originally thought that Fox worked for us," conservative commentator David Frum has observed, "and now we are discovering we work for Fox." This turned out to be literally true in the case of at least four likely Republican candidates for president in 2012: Sarah Palin, Mike Huckabee, Newt Gingrich, and Rick Santorum. In fact, as two *Politico* writers observed in the autumn of 2010, "with the exception of Mitt Romney, Fox now has deals with every major potential Republican presidential candidate not currently in elected office."

In the first place, one must note the oddity of this situation. After all, what are political candidates doing working for a "news" station? Isn't that inconsistent with the very idea of journalism? Can these candidates be trusted to tell the truth about themselves, their supporters, and their opponents? What's more, why, exactly, would these candidates want to give a single cable station such exclusive access?

Politico quoted C-SPAN political editor Steve Scully explaining that when C-SPAN tried to interview Sarah Palin, "he was told he had to first get Fox's permission—which the network, citing her contract, ultimately denied. Producers at NBC, ABC, CBS, CNN, and MSNBC all report similar experiences." "We have tried to book many of them, but they have always refused, saying they are exclusive to Fox," explained another rival network staffer.

Politico also noted that when these candidates appear on Fox, they simply "offer their views on issues of the day" without challenge or correction. As of September 2010, potential Republican presidential candidates had made 269 appearances on the station. Fox is paying the candidates it pretends to cover, and this protects them having to answer questions from any honest or unbiased journalist. "We're acutely aware of this," explained a "Fox insider" to *Politico*, and yet "the cold reality is, nobody at the reporter level has any say on this," added "another source familiar with the inner workings of Fox."

And this cozy arrangement sure works for the candidates, who not only rake in cash but also are protected from answering any uncomfortable questions. Why else would Sarah Palin tell Delaware GOP Senate nominee Christine O'Donnell to stick to Fox (and do so while on Fox)? "She's gonna have to dismiss that, go with her gut, get out there, speak to the American people, speak through Fox News, and let the independents who are tuning into you, let them know what it is that she stands for, the principles behind her positions," Palin explained.

These candidates are not the only ones to enjoy a Fox perch. Karl Rove also enjoys a regular Rupert Murdoch paycheck. And again, the relationship between Rove and journalism is tangential at best, hostile at worst. For instance, not long ago Fox News's Alisyn Camerota interviewed Rove and committed one of those faux pas that can make viewing Fox so interesting. She asked him about the steady stream of protesters from the antiwar organization Code Pink who had been following him on his book tour. "These are sort of sad and pathetic people," Rove explained. "Let's not give them any more attention." How dare a journalist ask an inconvenient question of a paid employee of the very same news organization!

Bringing Rove into the equation naturally raises the issue of Fox and political contributions. As *New York Times* reporter Jim Rutenberg explains, "Already a prominent presence as an analyst on Fox News Channel and a columnist at The Wall Street Journal, Mr. Rove is also playing a leading role in building what amounts to a shadow Republican Party, a network of donors and operatives that is among the most aggressive in the Republican effort to capture control of the House and the Senate." In addition to plans for "an anti-Democratic barrage of attack ads that will be run tens of thousands of times, a final get-out-the-vote push with some 40 million negative mail pieces, and 20 million automated phone calls," Rove sought to guide both voters and operatives in picking the party's candidates. When he guessed wrong on just how nutty Republican primary voters were likely to be regarding the Republican Senate primary in Delaware, Rutenberg reports, "his stance prompted blistering criticism from activists and Ms. Palin, who, in a 'woodshed moment' clearly directed at least in part at Mr. Rove during a recent speech in Iowa, called for party unity, asking, 'Did you ever lose a big game growing up?'" Rove quickly reversed himself.

The single best place for Rove and for the candidates to scare up contributors is by pitching themselves to Fox viewers. Delaware Tea Party candidate Christine O'Donnell reportedly told Republican Party insiders who resisted her candidacy "that she has 'Sean Hannity in my back pocket, and I can go on his show and raise money by attacking you guys.'" The *Las Vegas Sun* has acquired audio of Nevada Republican Senate candidate Sharron Angle explaining the following to a guest at a house party in her honor:

GUEST: Sharron, how are you doing as far as the fund-raising?
SHARRON ANGLE: It's going really well. Here's the deal: When I get a friendly press outlet—not so much the guy that's interviewing me—it's their audience that I'm trying to reach. I'm going on Bill O'Reilly the 16th. They say, "Bill O'Reilly, you better watch

out for that guy; he's not necessarily a friendly." Doesn't matter, his audience is friendly, and if I can get an opportunity to say that at least once on his show—when I said it on Sean Hannity's television show we made $40,000 before we even got out of the studio in New York. It was just [great]. So that's what I'm really reaching out to is that audience. [In August, Angle added, in an interview with Fox News that she expected the media "to ask the questions we want to answer, so that they report the news the way we want it reported." She sure picked the right place.]

Although Fox purports to keep its own employees off the Republican fund-raising circuit, a Media Matters investigation demonstrates beyond any doubt that such appearances are business as usual at the network, saying, "At least twenty Fox News personalities have endorsed, raised money for or campaigned for Republican candidates or causes, or against Democratic candidates or causes, in more than 300 instances and in at least 49 states," and they have been routinely advertised as Fox News personalities while doing so. No wonder Palin shouted out at one of her rallies, "What would we do without Fox News, America? We love our Fox News."

No line separates right-wing Republican Party propaganda and the "news" broadcast on Fox. Indeed, when Fox's parent corporation, News Corp, gave a $1.25 million donation to the Republican Governors Association and another $1 million to the pseudo-Republican U.S. Chamber of Commerce during the 2010 election cycle, the cash was undoubtedly much appreciated but was in many respects redundant. Fox, like much of the Murdoch media empire, has more in common with the integrated political/judicial/business/media empire that is making a mockery of Italian democracy under the rule of Prime Minister Silvio Berlusconi than it does with any American media organization. It is a 24/7 continuous contribution to the conservative cause in America, with a market capitalization of more than $43 billion, an operating income during the first quarter of 2010 of $1.15 billion, and a budget for the Fox News channel of over $1.2 billion.

Ask yourself these questions:

- Would a genuine news network reproduce a Republican press release, replete with typos?
- Would a genuine news network run, over a five-day period, twenty-two excerpts from health care forums in which every single speaker was opposed?
- Would a genuine news network allow a producer to cheerlead, off camera, anti-Obama protesters?
- Would a genuine news network take out full-page ads to complain of insufficient coverage of antigovernment protest marches it had promoted?
- Would a genuine news network run the following headlines trumpeted above the caption "Fox Nation Victory"?

> "SENATE REMOVES 'END OF LIFE' PROVISION"
> "CONGRESS DELAYS HEALTH CARE RATIONING BILL"
> "ANTI–TEA PARTY REPORTER DUMPED BY CNN"
> "OBAMA'S DRIVE FOR CLIMATE CHANGE BILL DELAYED"
> "OBAMA'S 'GREEN CZAR' RESIGNS"

Is it any wonder that according to survey after survey Fox News viewers, despite their obsessive interest, are among the worst-informed Americans about politics? A study by Democracy Corps finds that this audience believes "Obama is deliberately and ruthlessly advancing a 'secret agenda' to bankrupt our country and dramatically expand government control over all aspects of our daily lives," with the ultimate goal of "the destruction of the United States as it was conceived by our founders and developed over the past 200 years." And it's not just Fox's audience that is the problem because so much of the misinformation

Fox promulgates seeps unfiltered into the rest of the MSM. Remember the "death panel" craze of summer 2009? That August an NBC News/*Wall Street Journal* poll found that 45 percent of Americans thought the reform proposals would likely allow "the government to make decisions about when to stop providing medical care to the elderly." As E. J. Dionne points out, "A straight-out lie influenced the course of one of our most important debates," and it was repeatedly and knowingly trumpeted on Fox.

The network also serves an additional function: It keeps Republicans in line. During the period in 2010 when Republican senator Lindsey Graham (SC) was negotiating to join Democrat John Kerry (MA) and conservative independent Joe Lieberman (CT) in their attempt to craft an energy bill, Graham warned Lieberman and Kerry that they needed to get as far as they could in negotiating the bill "before Fox News got wind of the fact that this was a serious process," one of the people involved in the negotiations said. "He would say, 'The second they focus on us, it's gonna be all cap-and-tax all the time, and it's gonna become just a disaster for me on the airwaves. We have to move this along as quickly as possible.'" It's not hard to discern who was boss in the Fox/Republican relationship.

THE TICKING TIME BOMB

Fox's all-but-official sponsorship of the Tea Party movement, its ginning up of anti-Obama protesters both on and off camera, and the willingness of its hosts to put forth the most irresponsible kinds of allegations and accusations in an atmosphere that is already thick with the threat of violence directed toward America's first black president are truly shocking and scary developments in the history of media. The cumulative effect of such reports can be seen in the August 2010 finding that 24 percent of Americans questioned had somehow come to the conclusion that the United States of America elected a Black Muslim to the presidency in 2008; this was nearly double the almost-as-incredible number who had thought this to be true in March 2009. What's more, almost 50 percent said they were not certain just what religion Obama was. Fully 60 percent of those who believed that Obama prayed facing Mecca cited "the media" as their source.

Not only did Fox frequently invite guests on its programs who insisted that Obama was, in fact, Muslim; the network's hosts also grew obsessive in their desire to inflame fear and hatred of American citizens who actually were. The controversy over "Park51"—the Islamic cultural center proposed for downtown New York City two blocks away from where the Twin Towers once stood—might never have happened had it not been for the hysteria that Fox, together with the Murdoch-owned *New York Post*, purposely set out to inspire. They were happy to lie to their audience to achieve this goal. To take just three of many, many potential examples, in late August 2010 Fox News host Bill O'Reilly said the proposed center's leader, Imam Feisal Abdul Rauf, a U.S. citizen who had already spent twenty-five years working to improve relations between the Muslim world and the United States, was "no friend to America" because his "radical" views were "very disturbing." Fellow Fox host Glenn Beck falsely claimed that Rauf was "connected to" Hamas and that Rauf employed an anti-Semitic imam. Sean Hannity claimed that Rauf wished to "shred our Constitution" and install "Sharia law [*sic*] as the law of the land in America."

In fact, Imam Rauf was exactly the kind of Muslim leader that U.S. conservatives professed to admire. He specifically condemned "the death cult of al-Qaeda and its adherent." He worked with the Bush administration by undertaking diplomatic missions on its behalf and consulted with the FBI on counterterrorism efforts. Regarding U.S. laws, he said in his book *What's Right with Islam*, "Many Muslims regard the form of government that the American founders established a little over two centuries ago as the form of governance that best expresses Islam's original values and principles."

But in the midst of the wholly manufactured media frenzy over
this proposed cultural center, Fox hosts routinely equated law-abiding
American Muslims with terrorists, with communists, even with Nazis.
In fact, Fox's hosts drove themselves so crazy over the danger posed to
America by law-abiding Muslims that they even slandered the man
who happened to be the second-largest stockholder (after Murdoch
himself) in Fox's parent company, News Corp. Prince Alwaleed bin
Talal of Saudi Arabia owns 7 percent, or roughly $3 billion at this
writing, of Murdoch's company, which in turn owns 9 percent of bin
Talal's Arabic-language entertainment company, Rotana. Without
mentioning his name or his relationship with News Corp, Fox News
contributor Dan Senior complained that bin Talal's "Kingdom
Foundation . . . you know, is this Saudi organization, headed up by
the guy that tried to give Rudy Giuliani $10 million after 9/11 that
was sent back, funds radical madrassas all over the world." "And he
funds this imam," Fox host Brian Kilmeade added. As Jon Stewart
noted, by this logic patriotic Americans should boycott Fox as well,
which perhaps explains the network's reluctance to alert viewers either
to the name of "the guy" or to the fact that his billions were in part responsible for paying the salaries of Fox commentators. (True to form,
the insinuations aired on Fox against its own second-largest investor
had no demonstrable basis in available evidence. Bin Talal later told
the *New York Times* that he had "nothing to do with" the Park51 center and did not even support its construction.)

Nor is it likely just a coincidence that while this hate-mongering
was being broadcast, according to the same newspaper, "a record
number of Muslim workers [were] complaining of employment discrimination, from co-workers calling them 'terrorist' or 'Osama' to
employers barring them from wearing head scarves or taking prayer
breaks." When Nevada Republican senatorial candidate Sharron
Angle complained that cities like Dearborn, Michigan, and
Frankford, Texas, were living through the horror of a "militant

terrorist situation" and Oklahoma state senator Rex Duncan introduced an amendment to the state constitution to prevent what he called the "storm on the horizon," by which he meant the "looming threat" of the introduction of Islamic law into Oklahoma, it is not hard to imagine in whose audience these demagogues were finding their supporters.

"A DEEP-SEATED HATRED FOR WHITE PEOPLE"

According to a study by the Pew Project on Excellence in Journalism, right-wing talk radio enjoys 48 million regular listeners, which is not only many times Fox's audience but also more than twice the collective audience for the three TV network evening news shows combined, more than five times the audience of the three network Sunday news shows, nearly seven times the combined audience for cable news shows, and, sadly, nearly ten times the audience for National Public Radio's *Morning Edition* and *All Things Considered*. (It is also, alas, sixteen times the audience for Jon Stewart and Stephen Colbert.) And the consistency of its message is hard to miss. To pick just one day at random, on April 10, 2010, at 3:15 PM, I happen to click on the Web site of the *Drudge Report*. Here's what I saw near the top of the page:

GINGRICH: Obama 'most radical president ever'

LIMBAUGH: Obama 'inflicting untold damage on this great country'

MARK LEVIN: Obama 'Closest Thing to Dictator We've Ever Had'

PALIN: Obama's 'vast nuclear experience he acquired' community organizer

LIZ CHENEY: Obama Putting America on 'Path to Decline'

HANNITY: Obama 'Is a Socialist'

SAVAGE: 'Obama the Destroyer'

Fox's Glenn Beck is a particularly useful vehicle for examining the nexus between Fox and right-wing hate radio, which not only excites so many Tea Party types but also spills into mainstream reporting. When Beck posits that Obama "has a deep-seated hatred for white people, or white culture," including, say, his mother and the grandparents who raised him, Beck sounds like a madman to most of us. But not only do his views represent a consensus among many of his Fox colleagues and viewers; they also were actually endorsed by the network owner, Rupert Murdoch. But between Beck's television program and his even less restrained daily radio broadcast, Fox is supporting the spreading of some genuinely worrisome, potentially violence-inducing arguments against America's president. Beck feels no compunction in terming the president the leader of an "army of thugs" and comparing the country under his presidency to "the damn Planet of the Apes." Beck has promoted a 1936 book, *The Red Network*, written by Elizabeth Dilling, in which the author claims that "un-Christianized" "colored people" are "savages" and that "American Negroes have acquired professions, property, banks, homes, and produced a rising class of refined, home loving people" thanks to the "American government and the inspiration of Christianity."

It's impossible to say to what degree overt racism against a black man with a foreign-sounding name mixes with the hostility on display on Fox, on talk radio, at Tea Party rallies, and elsewhere in right-wing America. Most Americans and all media personalities are sufficiently sophisticated about the way the world works to deny having a racist bone in their bodies. Nevertheless, when former House Majority Leader Tom DeLay said he thought it would be a good idea if, instead of the normal inauguration ceremonies, Barack Obama had "a nice little chicken dinner, and we'll save the $125 million," DeLay was sending a not-terribly carefully coded signal to white racists. Ditto Fox TV host Laura Ingraham, whose best-selling book, purporting to be Obama's diary, made much of an imaginary addiction to ribs by Michelle Obama.

That such respectable personalities could traffic in such tropes without any noticeable negative impact on their careers was yet another unspoken victory for Murdoch, Beck, and "Fox Nation."

Erich Boehlert of Media Matters describes an incident during the summer of 2010 precipitated by Beck. For more than a year prior to the incident, Beck had focused on the allegedly nefarious activities of a small, progressive foundation called the Tides Center. In thirty separate broadcasts, Beck portrayed the center, which provides administrative services such as payroll, benefits, and insurance to myriad small and start-up organizations fighting for social change, as "a central player in a larger, nefarious cabal of Marxist/socialist/Nazi Obama-loving outlets determined to destroy democracy in America," in Boehlert's words. Tides, Beck informed his audience, was staffed by "thugs" and "bullies" committed to "the nasty of the nastiest," like indoctrinating schoolchildren and undoubtedly creating a "mass organization to seize power." In response to Beck's provocations, a gentleman named Byron Williams left his home in Northern California to travel to the Tides Foundation; he had with him enough guns and ammunition to murder the entire staff. This would, he believed, spark a right-wing political revolution. He was motivated, his mother explained, by the TV news he watched, which demonstrated how "Congress was railroading through all these left-wing agenda." In a jailhouse interview, Williams explained that Beck "blew [his] mind, giving him "every ounce of evidence that [he] could possibly need" to make his decision to turn terrorist. Fortunately, California Highway Patrol officers pulled Williams over on a DUI charge. When Williams opened fire on the cops, a shootout ensued and his plans for domestic terrorism were upended.

Sad to say, such talk is nothing unusual for Beck. Among many, many other examples, Beck has

- suggested that Obama is pushing America toward civil war and deliberately "trying to destroy the country."

- capped two weeks of violent fear-mongering about progressives by warning that when their attempts at a "soft revolution" fail, eventually progressives "just start shooting people."
- said the "people around the president" support "armed insurrection" and "bombing."
- repeatedly insinuated that the Obama administration will kill him.
- used a quote from Thomas Jefferson to warn about coming "rivers of blood."
- compared himself to "Israeli Nazi hunters" and announced that "to the day I die, I am going to be a progressive hunter."
- included in his advice to Liberty University grads that they should "shoot to kill" and that graduates "have a responsibility" to speak out, or "blood . . . will be on our hands."
- informed viewers that the "world is on edge" and said that "those who survive" will "stand in the truth" and "listen."
- said that some progressive groups don't have "a problem with blood in the streets."
- claimed that the present day will seem like good times "when we're behind barbed wire and just eating rock soup."

In mid-November 2010, Beck took a somewhat surprising step deeper into the right-wing swamps of ignorance and prejudice he often inhabits with a special two-part show devoted to attacking the liberal, Hungarian-American billionaire George Soros. During the course of a complicated explication of Soros's alleged activities as a "puppet-master," Beck—to the shame of everyone involved with production and broadcast of his program—engaged in some of the most offensive anti-Semitic imagery ever purposely shown on American TV. The fact that he did this while accusing Soros, who had to flee the

Nazis, of aiding the Nazis against his fellow Jews, only added to the absurdity. Beck calls Soros his own "shadow government" happily manipulating his "puppet" Barack Obama. He actually equated Soros's effort in helping democratic revolutions succeed in overthrowing Communism in Europe with evidence that Soros seeks to take over the United States of America. "Not only does he want to bring America to her knees, financially, he wants to reap obscene profits off us as well," Beck insisted. These notions, and the imagery they evoke, of an unpatriotic Jewish financier who is somehow manipulating governments and world currencies for his own nefarious purposes, could have come directly out of the Nazi playbook. As Michelle Goldberg wrote in the *Daily Beast*, Beck's show was little more than a "symphony of anti-Semitic dog-whistles. Nothing like it has ever been on American television before." And yet, Murdoch and the entire News Corporation empire continued to stand by him.

Beck and Fox not only ran interference for Tea Party conservatives during their ascent through the media during Obama's first year in office; the entire network also pretty much turned itself into the Tea Party's official propaganda organ. On July 28, 2009, for instance, Fox Nation posted a promotional ad for the Tea Party Express using the headline "Will You Join the Tea Party Express?" The August 19, 2009, edition of *Fox & Friends* hosted Tea Party spokesman Mark Williams to explain, in cohost Brian Kilmeade's words, "how you can join" Williams and company's then-upcoming national bus tour. During the segment, Fox News aired graphics noting the dates and locations of twenty-two tour stops. On the October 25 edition of *Fox & Friends Sunday*, cohost Dave Briggs described the Tea Party Express by saying that "the bus tour that took the country by storm is back by popular demand." This continued throughout the fall. And yet, though the network frequently hosted Williams, it gave no hint of his racial views, on display in any number of blog posts and overtly racist statements, such as those that contained the "newly discovered letter" he pretended to unearth from NAACP president "Precious Ben Jealous" to President Abraham Lincoln. It read, in part:

> We Colored People have taken a vote and decided that we don't cotton to that whole emancipation thing. Freedom means having to work for real, think for ourselves, and take consequences along with the rewards. That is just far too much to ask of us Colored People and we demand that it stop!
>
> [. . .]
>
> And the ridiculous idea of "reduc[ing] the size and intrusiveness of government." What kind of massa would ever not want to control my life? As Coloreds we must have somebody care for us otherwise we would be on our own, have to think for ourselves and make decisions!
>
> [. . .]
>
> Mr. Lincoln, you were the greatest racist ever. We had a great gig. Three squares, room and board, all our decisions made by the massa in the house. Please repeal the 13th and 14th Amendments and let us get back to where we belong.

AN EMPIRE OF THEIR OWN

But even to focus on so significant a force as Fox is to miss an entire forest for a few trees. The News Corp empire is vast and wide, and it deliberately slants the news while shamelessly promoting blatant disinformation in platform after platform all over the world. Murdoch controls so many media properties in so many places that the notion of focusing on one single donation to one group might be considered trivial by comparison. The entire empire is at the disposal of political conservatism. Ask yourself, Why does News Corp continue to publish a newspaper, the *New York Post*, that loses—according to Murdoch family sources—in the area of $50 million a year? Is it because the company is so proud of its terrible tabloid? On the other, more re-spectable end of the far-right spectrum from Fox one finds its most significant recent money-losing acquisition: the *Wall Street Journal*.

For decades, in the days before Murdoch's takeover of Dow Jones Corporation, which owns the newspaper, the *Journal*'s conservative edi-torials benefited from being placed in a newspaper that was a must-read for the nation's business community. The authority of its often-excellent news pages gave a certain gravitas to opinions that would oth-erwise have been considered quirky at best, nutty and irresponsible at worst. Today, however, the political spectrum has shifted so far to the right that the oddball ravings in the paper's opinion pages are consid-ered comfortably within the spectrum of responsible opinion.

By inserting the irresponsible views of right-wing talk radio, Fox News, and Tea Party agitators into respectable discourse, the *Journal* editorial pages have become yet another valuable weapon in the con-servative quiver. When someone who was once as respected and ad-mired across all political lines as Johns Hopkins professor Fouad Ajami sounds like Rush Limbaugh on the newspaper's pages about what he deemed, not thirteen months into Obama's presidency, to be the unhappy "un-American moment in our history" that gave rise to Barack Obama's election, this is a victory for thoughtlessness itself. Gone was "the empiricism in political life that had marked the American temper in politics," Ajami argued, apparently seriously, in the wake of George W. Bush's fantasy presidency. "A charismatic leader had risen in a manner akin to the way politics plays out in dis-tressed and Third World societies," Ajami went on. Obama, Ajami maintained, had interpreted the election "as a plebiscite granting him a writ to remake the basic political compact of this republic" and had "overwhelmed all restraint."

The influence of this unmistakable attempt to challenge Obama's legitimacy in so high profile a forum, together with countless other ex-amples like it (remember, Karl Rove is also a weekly *Wall Street Journal* columnist), presents a barrier to Obama and his agenda that no president has faced before. Not even the same paper's hysterical campaign against Bill Clinton can compare because it was undertaken when the far-right media were much weaker and the MSM much stronger. (The editors followed not long afterward with another anti-Obama op-ed by page staffer Dorothy Rabinowitz titled, I kid you not, "The Alien in the White House.")

The best-known *Journal* editorial writer is another ex-Republican flack, Peggy Noonan, who also doubles as a frequent talking head on Sunday news programs. As far as I can tell, she is considered to be perhaps the most reasonable regular contributor to the page. Noonan has an interesting prose style, which floats above the real world in a mystical cloud of self-absorption that is similar, but not in a good way, to the way Jerry Garcia's guitar solos used to float over Grateful Dead songs without actually entering them. One of Noonan's August 2010 columns began with a lengthy excerpt from a previous column during which time she had noted that "the temperature in the world was very high." (This being the *Journal*, she was not talking about the world's climate, which was doing just fine, scientific evidence notwithstanding.) I never was genuinely confident that I understood the actual topic of the column, but my interest lay more in its perspective than in its putative topic. At one point Noonan observed, parenthetically, "(Who is the most self-punishing person in America right now? The person who didn't do well during the abundance)." Like her editors, Noonan appeared unaware that just about all American wage workers fell into this category. To cite just one statistic, the U.S. worker's average hourly wage, according to the 2006 *Economic Report of the President*, fell, in constant 1982 dollars, from $8.21 in 1967 to $8.17 in 2005, while during the previous quarter-century the portion of the national income accruing to the richest 1 percent of Americans had doubled, the share going to the richest 0.1 percent had tripled, and the share going to the richest 0.01 percent had quadrupled.

Turning to immigration, Noonan wrote, "The federal government continues its standoff with the state of Arizona over how to handle illegal immigration. The point of view of our thoughtful leaders is, in general, that borders that are essentially open are good, or not so bad. The point of view of those on the ground who are anxious about our nation's future, however, is different, more like: 'We live in a welfare state and we've just expanded health care. Unemployment's up. Could we sort of calm down, stop illegal immigration, and absorb what we've got?'" This was a rather odd way of characterizing both sides. After all, the Obama administration was at the time deporting a record number of undocumented immigrants convicted of crimes and accelerating the pace of deportations overall. U.S. immigration authorities deported 392,862 people in 2009, an increase of approximately 81,000 over the previous year under the Bush administration. (About half, 195,772, were said to be convicted criminals.) The Obama administration was also in the process of sending National Guard units, armed with unmanned drones, to police the border. Days after Noonan's column appeared, the Department of Homeland Security announced it was expanding its Secure Communities program to all twenty-five counties along the U.S.-Mexico border—a program that required local law enforcement to give the fingerprint files it collected to immigration officials, who were then directed to begin removal proceedings. What's more, at the time Noonan wrote these words, the United States was actually experiencing negative net immigration from Mexico, owing to the economic downturn. Not that anyone would know it from the hysteria that surrounds the issue, and apparently infected Noonan's thinking, but between March 2007 and March 2009 the United States actually experienced a net outflow of about 1 million undocumented workers, or 8 percent of those who had previously been here. Her logic is further undermined by the fact that Judge Susan Bolton of the Federal District Court of Arizona found the state's law to be unconstitutional owing not only to its encroachment on federal responsibilities but also to "a substantial likelihood that officers will wrongfully arrest legal resident aliens." "By enforcing this statute, Arizona would impose," she said, citing a previous Supreme Court case, a "distinct, unusual and extraordinary burden on legal resident aliens." This was hardly a "sort of calm down, stop illegal immigration, and absorb what we've got." (And let us note before leaving the issue Noonan's apparently innocent belief that the United States can simply "stop" illegal immigration anytime it so decides or that Arizona's measures are likely to be effective in that regard.)

One can apply such analysis to just about any Peggy Noonan column. In her July 30, 2010, column, for instance, she wrote, "It's a sign of Democratic panic that a week ago they were saying what was wrong with the GOP was they have no plan, while now what's wrong is that they do have one." Is it possible that Noonan is unaware of a third possibility: that even though the Republicans might have come up with a "plan" of sorts, it might, in fact, be worthy of criticism?

In another summer 2010 column, this one on the need for a "wise man" or two to come save the day, her nominations for this prestigious, albeit imaginary appointment were Senator Tom Coburn (R-OK), Governor Haley Barbour (R-MS), and Governor Mitch Daniels (R-IN). Let's take them one by one. Tom Coburn protested the television broadcast of *Schindler's List* because television had been taken "to an all-time low, with full-frontal nudity, violence and profanity." He described the airing as "irresponsible sexual behavior." He is also the fellow who warned about "rampant" lesbianism in rural Oklahoma. As I write these words, he is, according to my morning newspaper, exercising his wisdom to prevent the speedy passage of legislation to fix many of the flaws in the nation's food safety system—although a bill to do so "has broad bipartisan support, is a priority for the Obama administration and has the backing of both industry and consumer groups"—unless the rather trivial costs of the bill were made up by spending reductions. (A Coburn spokesperson also explained

that the senator had expressed doubts that expanding the authority of
the Food and Drug Administration would "result in improved food
safety.") That bill passed in the Sentate on November 30, 2010, 73–25
as Reid went to the trouble to break the hold. Haley Barbour, who
was, at the moment of Noonan's column, exploring a run at the
Republican nomination for president, has been a paid lobbyist for
both the tobacco and gambling industries. And Mitch Daniels, who is
also a potential Republican candidate for president, was director of the
Office of Management and Budget under George W. Bush at a time
when government surpluses turned into some of the largest deficits in
U.S. history.

Alas, none of these efforts scales the heights reached by Noonan's
infamous "magic dolphin" column crafted during the "Elián
González" episode of 2000. Recall that back then a group of conservative Miami Cubans did not wish to return to his father in Cuba a
young child whose mother had been killed at sea. With the support of
the very same "family values" supporters among U.S. conservatives,
Noonan insisted that her hero, and former employer, Ronald Reagan
would never have allowed his Justice Department to enforce the law
and the court's decision to return the child. Moreover, he "would not
have dismissed the story of the dolphins [sent by God to rescue Elián,
according to some of the young boy's protectors/kidnappers] as
Christian kitsch, but seen it as possible evidence of the reasonable assumption that God's creatures had been commanded to protect one of
God's children." She concluded, "But then he was a man."

The *Journal*, in the tradition of doctrinaire Stalinism, makes no
distinction between art and politics as its arts and culture pages—and
particularly its book reviews—reflect all of the political prejudices of
its editorial board. Take a look, for instance, at an August 16, 2010, review by James K. Glassman of a book by Thomas Geoghegan called
Were You Born on the Wrong Continent? According to the reviewer, the
book was a "meandering stream of consciousness" by "an admitted

nonexpert" who "details various boring conversations he had with anonymous Germans and Frenchmen he bumped into, drops a few statistics, cites some books and comes to the conclusion that we Americans would lead richer lives if only we adopted European social and economic policy—especially the part about high taxes." Glassman rebuked the author by arguing that "Europe's economic story in recent years—well before the current crisis—has been one of sluggish growth and high unemployment. As a result, a wide gap has opened up between Europe and the U.S. in the most revealing indicator of economic well-being, GDP [gross domestic product] per capita."

This is an old story and one Antonio Gramsci would appreciate. Conservatives have been making exactly these arguments for decades. "If you want a lower standard of living," conservative policy experts Grace-Marie Turner and Robert Moffit argued in a December 2006 op-ed piece, "the Europeans have the right prescription." Their argument echoes views popular across the conservative spectrum, from *Newsweek*'s Robert Samuelson ("Europe is history's has-been"), to *National Review*'s Jonah Goldberg ("Europe has an asthmatic economy"), to *New York Times* pundit David Brooks ("The European model is flat-out unsustainable"). And yet, somehow, these same European nations have by almost every measurement—individual rights and community, capitalist enterprise and social solidarity, and even personal mobility—proved superior to the United States.

As it happens, *Newsweek* published a cover story the same day this *Journal* review appeared in which it ranked the quality of life in nations across the globe based on five categories of national well-being—education, health, quality of life, economic competitiveness, and political environment—and compiled metrics within these categories across one hundred nations. The United States did not even make it into the top ten. Finland was number one, and most of the rest were also in Europe, particularly northern Europe, where tax rates are highest. For instance, Americans work an average of 1,841 hours per years, whereas Germans work 1,473 hours. Yet 24.7 percent of the elderly and 21.9 percent of children in the United States fall below 50 percent of median income, compared to 10.1 percent of the elderly and 9 percent of children in Germany. France, Germany, and Sweden provide paid maternity leave, paid paternity leave, expanded holidays, shorter workweeks, and nursing home benefits. The United States provides none of these benefits.

Millions more readers will see Glassman's distortions rather than Geoghegan's arguments. The myths the review purposely perpetuates will be consistent with the propaganda people receive in so many other places, like Fox News. And so the circle will be complete, and no one will even have to address the fact of so much European success and so much American failure in providing the majority of citizens with the health, housing, and economic security necessary to pursue "happiness" in a meaningful way. And any attempt by Barack Obama to introduce European-style security measures into the economy will be met by a similar combination of disdain and dismissal based on smug ignorance and conceited condescension of the type demonstrated by Glassman et al. (Ironically, Glassman's bio describes him as a "former under secretary of state for public diplomacy and public affairs" and the "executive director of the George W. Bush Institute in Dallas." All true, but the man is too modest. Glassman is also the author of the infamous work *Dow 36,000: The New Strategy for Profiting from the Coming Rise in the Stock Market,* published not long before the tech bubble of the 1990s brought the Dow a great deal closer to 6,000 than it ever got to Glassman's prediction. At this writing the Dow Jones average stands at less than one-third of Glassman's prediction.)

Despite the presence of Noonan, Rove, Glassman, and company, it is perhaps in the area of unsigned editorials where the *Journal* is both most damaging and most dishonest. Compare, for instance, two pieces, one written in the immediate aftermath of the September 11, 2001, attacks and one published in the spring of 2010. In the first the editors insisted that President Bush get to work immediately exploiting the attacks for political gain. They demanded that Bush "spend his windfall of political capital" resulting from the attacks by, among other things, replacing what was then a significant government annual surplus of around $150 billion with what they called "pro-growth tax cuts," or those aimed at corporations and the wealthy. The *Journal* editors warned against the "temptation . . . to settle for a lowest common denominator stimulus, for the sake of bipartisanship." But this was only the beginning. "The transformed political landscape should also boost other Bush initiatives," the editors argued. They went on to declare that Bush should use the attacks to demand more offshore oil drilling, greater authority to negotiate free-trade agreements, approval of all of Bush's nominees to various offices, and a whole host of other things that had nothing whatever to do with protecting America from terrorism. Meanwhile, under Barack Obama, one could find the editors making an almost perfectly contrary argument. Beneath the words "A crisis is a terrible thing to exploit," *Journal* editors took the president to task for having the temerity to exploit the financial crisis of 2008 for political gain. Obama's problem, they insisted, was that "Democrats have committed the classic political mistake of ideological overreach," as if ideological overreach were not exactly what the editors were demanding of George Bush's right-wing government in the wake of the mass murder of 3,000 Americans. Given the disappearance of so many once serious outlets and the diminution of others, these ravings have assumed a central place in the nation's political discourse.

Although the left media structure is not as weak as it was entering the Bush years, it does not compare with the Murdoch empire, much less the entire structure of right-wing propaganda masquerading as news. True, MSNBC now features three hours of primetime liberal programming. The blogosphere has given birth to any number of progressive journalistic enterprises, like Huffington Post and Josh

Marshall's terrific Talking Points Memo (TPM), which together with hundreds of less famous enterprises have helped inform those interested in facts and patterns of political behavior hitherto unnoticed by MSM reporters. Wealthy liberal funders banded together under the auspices of the Democracy Alliance to ensure secure funding for influential new institutions such as the Center for American Progress (where I've been a senior fellow since 2003) and Media Matters for America (which published my "Altercation" web blog between 2006 and 2008)—just two of the many worthy efforts to inject sensible center-left policy proposals into the debate, in the case of the former, and to correct conservative misinformation, in the case of the latter. Even so, all of these new groups added together do not begin to approach the scale of Fox, talk radio, and the Heritage Foundation, the American Enterprise Institute, the Hoover Institution, and the rest of the right-wing counterestablishment. Neither does the recent rise of the "netroots" online, however welcome this development may be.

The *Journal's* role in helping to make Fox "kosher" for the rest of the media is undeniably important. (Fox even hosts the editor's regular Friday night television program, originally developed at taxpayer expense and hosted by the alleged bastion of far-left radical politics, the Public Broadcasting Service [PBS].) No less important is the unwillingness of those in the more respectable precincts of the mainstream media to admit the distinction between allegedly objective journalism and Fox's brand of naked propaganda.

And yet when, in the autumn of 2009 interim White House communications director Anita Dunn explained that the White House now planned to treat Fox "the way we would treat an opponent," adding that because the network had "undertak[en] a war against Barack Obama and the White House, we don't need to pretend that this is the way that legitimate news organizations behave," most MSM journalists rushed to Fox's defense. *Washington Post* media reporter Howard Kurtz equated the Obama administration's reaction to Fox with John Kennedy's complaints about the *Herald Tribune*, Lyndon Johnson's unhappiness with the *New York Times*, and various Republican attacks on the media, finding it to be "no surprise that the Obama White House isn't happy with its coverage and is battling back." *Baltimore Sun* critic David Zurawik actually professed to hear "echoes of Nixon-Agnew" in the Obama White House and accused the administration of failing to respect "press freedom." ABC's Jake Tapper complained to White House briefer Robert Gibbs, "It's escaped none of our notice that the White House has decided in the last few weeks to declare one of our sister organizations 'not a news organization' and to tell the rest of us not to treat them like a news organization. Can you explain why it's appropriate for the White House to decide that a news organization is not one?" That Tapper could not see how the Fox News network differed from his own was sad but telling. Obama adviser David Axelrod was forced, while appearing on ABC's *This Week*, to school Tapper's colleague, George Stephanopoulos, about the reality that Fox was "really not news—it's pushing a point of view. And other news organizations like yours ought not to treat them that way."

And yet instead of objecting to the manner that Fox perverted the news for political purposes, the other networks appeared intent on aping it. This reflects one of the great unremarked successes of the conservative movement in recent decades: Its propaganda efforts, cloaked as journalistic enterprises, have so successfully inserted themselves into mainstream discourse and debate that conventional journalists are willing to embrace them without even realizing what is happening. Ask yourself, Why did the 2008 Democratic presidential debates—particularly those moderated by George Stephanopoulos and Charlie Gibson—focus so relentlessly on future tax rates affecting barely 5 percent of America's wealthiest citizens? And why did Stephanopoulos badger President Obama about whether the health care plan then under discussion constituted nothing more than a "tax increase" on the American people—a line that was immediately transposed into a

Republican National Committee attack ad the very next week? Why did CNN, which found it could no longer live with racist birther Lou Dobbs, rushed to hire the incendiary right-wing blogger Erick Erickson on the basis of such clever commentary as to call Michelle Obama a "Marxist harpy" and Supreme Court justice David Souter a "goat fucking child molester"? Why does MSNBC cohost Mika Brzezinski insist, rather crazily, on the day after Sarah Palin resigned her job as a governor to begin an estimated $20 million-plus-a-year career as a pundit and public speaker, that Palin represented "real Americans" as opposed to those who thought her quitting her job in the middle of her term worthy of criticism? Why does CNBC's Jim Cramer casually refer to the "Pelosi Politburo emasculation"? Why was racist Rush Limbaugh considered an appropriate roundtable commentator on NBC's *Meet the Press*? Why, indeed, was nutty Newt Gingrich—a man who claims to discern "a gay and secular fascism in this country that wants to impose its will on the rest of us"—the program's most popular guest in 2009, a year in which the presidency, the House, and the Senate were all controlled by Democrats. (Speaker of the House Nancy Pelosi did not even appear once; neither did any other former House speakers. In fact, no former House speaker other than Gingrich has ever appeared on *Meet the Press*.)

Remember, this favored sage of the mainstream media went so far in the autumn of 2010 as to embrace the bizarre arguments of right-wing journalist Dinesh D'Souza, published, unaccountably, on the cover of *Forbes* magazine, that President Obama "is so outside our comprehension, that only if you understand Kenyan, anti-colonial behavior, can you begin to piece together [his actions]?" D'Souza had written, "Incredibly, the U.S. is being ruled according to the dreams of a Luo tribesman of the 1950s. This philandering, inebriated African socialist, who raged against the world for denying him the realization of his anti-colonial ambitions, is now setting the nation's agenda through the reincarnation of his dreams in his son." (That his "travesty of an article . . . a fever dream of paranoia and irrationality" appeared in, much less on the cover of, a putatively respectable business magazine, as conservative writer Heather MacDonald observed, was "all too representative of the hysteria that now runs through a significant portion of the right-wing media establishment." She did not know at the time that the *Washington Post*'s op-ed page would open itself up to the D'Souza's "fever dreams" as well.) And yet according to Gingrich, appearing, yes, on *Meet the Press*, D'Souza's lunatic ravings had proved "the most accurate, predictive model for [President Obama's] behavior." He went on to call Obama "a person who is fundamentally out of touch with how the world works, who happened to have played a wonderful con, as a result of which he is now president." Such talk is not merely crazy but also deeply dangerous. After all, if what Gingrich and D'Souza say is true, what measures would not be justified in rescuing our country from this terrifying threat? It also inadvertently demonstrates the limitations of the MSM in playing their old-fashioned role as the gatekeepers of sanity, at the very least.

THE ATTACK ON ACORN

Then there's the ACORN affair. ACORN, or the Association of Community Organizations for Reform Now, was "founded in Little Rock in 1970 as an organization agitating for free school lunches, Vietnam veterans' rights and more hospital emergency rooms," as Harold Meyerson has explained, and grew "into the nation's largest community organizing group." In 2007, ACORN boasted field offices in one hundred cities with 260,000 members, located largely in inner-city minority communities. The organization helped to register more than 1.6 million voters between 2004 and 2008. In New York, one ACORN spin-off metamorphosed into the Working Families Party, now a state-wide liberal powerhouse. In 2004, in Florida, ACORN fought for and helped win a law that raised the state minimum wage. Before the organization's demise, its Web site described the association's mission as "to organize a majority constituency of low- to moderate-income people across the United States" to "take on issues of relevance to their communities, whether those issues are discrimination, affordable housing, a quality education, or better public services," and to encourage "low- to moderate-income members [to] act as leaders, spokespeople, and decision-makers within the organization." For these reasons alone, the actions of ACORN have probably long obsessed the far right in this country.

The manner in which it was successfully destroyed demonstrates decisively just how profoundly the mainstream media have been captured during the Obama presidency by the forces of the far right. The black political art of "working the refs" with constant and vociferous complaints of "liberal bias" in the media has a long and distinguished history. Few of its practitioners, however, succeeded so frequently—and nakedly—as the right-wing Web impresario and self-described ex–"Matt Drudge bitch" Andrew Breitbart. In the case of ACORN, albeit aided by the idiocy of a couple of low-level ACORN employees, Breitbart's underlings, the admitted criminal James O'Keefe and his associate Hannah Giles, lied to ACORN about their respective identities for the purpose of surreptitiously taping their words and actions and then releasing a doctored version of the tape to a credulous media, beginning with an exclusive viewing on Glenn Beck's Fox News show.

True to form, Breitbart snookered the MSM with the release of heavily edited videos of his associates' encounters at eight ACORN offices. O'Keefe falsely claimed that an undercover video campaign was part of a "nationwide ACORN child prostitution investigation" he had undertaken that would implicate numerous ACORN employees. But in at least six of those videotaped encounters, Breitbart's minions failed to tell the ACORN employees that they were planning to engage in child prostitution (or the ACORN employees refused to help them or contacted the police following their visit). Indeed, long after the damage had been done and ACORN was not only discredited but also defunded and ultimately destroyed, *New York Times* public editor Clark Hoyt did an extensive investigation in response to reader complaints and found that much of what the paper had reported as fact had turned out to be false. Moreover, an internal ACORN investigation undertaken by Scott Harshbarger, a former Massachusetts attorney general, and his associate, Amy Crafts, also found that the O'Keefe-Giles videos were heavily edited. Conversations were run out of sequence. Others were left out entirely, including those in the cities where ACORN employees called the police. The report found "no pattern of illegal conduct" by ACORN's employees—which does not in any way exonerate the actions of a few. These conclusions were consistent with the reports based on similar investigations, one by California attorney general Edmund G. Brown Jr. and another by Brooklyn district attorney Charles J. Hynes, who also found no illegal activity on ACORN's part. But as ACORN chief executive officer Bertha Lewis observed not long before her organization declared bankruptcy, "Our vindication on the facts doesn't necessarily pay the bills."

The simple fact of this story is that O'Keefe and company were lying and dissembling in order to advance their ideological agenda. Even so, it is perhaps not so surprising that many in the conservative media found such practices admirable. Ann Coulter called them "magnificent." *National Review* editor Rich Lowry said they deserved "an award for impactful guerilla journalism." Glenn Beck called Giles "courageous." Bill O'Reilly thought they deserved "congressional medals." Sean Hannity thought they were "journalistic pioneers." Andrew Breitbart, for whom O'Keefe worked, insisted that they "deserve[d] a Pulitzer Prize." (Fox News also repeatedly attempted to paint Obama as a tool of ACORN, owing to one lawsuit in which he had participated peripherally.)

Far more worrisome, however, was the fact that mainstream editors felt they needed to follow this lead and, indeed, criticized themselves and their colleagues for not doing so fast enough. Tom Rosenstiel of the Project for Excellence in Journalism explained, "Complaints by conservatives are slower to be picked up by non-ideological media because there are not enough conservatives and too many liberals in most newsrooms." *Washington Post* executive editor Marcus Brauchli worried, "We are not well-enough informed about conservative issues. It's particularly a problem in a town so dominated by Democrats and the Democratic point of view." The paper's ombudsman, Andrew Alexander, added that "traditional news outlets like The Post simply don't pay sufficient attention to conservative media or viewpoints." *New York Times* managing editor Jill Abramson fretted that her paper had demonstrated "insufficient tuned-in-ness to the issues that are dominating Fox News and talk radio."

Ask yourself why ABC's Stephanopoulos took up valuable time interviewing President Obama about the goings-on at ACORN given that U.S. grants to ACORN, already suspended at the time, accounted for less than one-thousandth of one percent of annual U.S. government spending. The president responded sensibly. "George, this is not the biggest issue facing the country. It's not something I'm paying a lot of attention to." But it was certainly something the entire media thought worth a great deal of attention.

The ACORN story is important not only as a cautionary tale but also because it plays a bizarrely large role in the right-wing narrative designed to undermine the legitimacy of the Obama presidency. As Peter Dreier of Occidental College and Christopher Martin of the University of Northern Iowa demonstrate in a detailed study entitled "Manipulating the Public Agenda: Why ACORN Was in the News and What the News Got Wrong," the far right has largely succeeded in framing the issue for much, if not all, of the mainstream media. The authors analyze the complete 2007–2008 coverage of ACORN by fifteen major news media organizations and the narrative frames of their 647 stories during that period. The study reveals a classic case of the agenda-setting effect of the news media: how a little-known organization became the subject of a major news story in the 2008 U.S. presidential campaign to such a degree that 82 percent of the respondents in an October 2008 national survey reported they had heard about ACORN. According to Dreier and Martin, virtually all of the coverage was one-sided, repeating the conservative criticisms of the group without seeking to verify them or provide ACORN or its supporters with a reasonable opportunity to respond to the allegations. Voter fraud was the dominant story line, with 55 percent of the 647 stories analyzed using it. (This narrative was most intense in the broadcast and cable media, with 68.7 percent of those stories deploying it.) Indeed, voter fraud may have been the only story frame about ACORN to which most news consumers were ever exposed. It is no wonder, therefore, that Republican presidential nominee John McCain felt himself to be on firm political ground in his third debate with Barack Obama despite making the fantastical claim that ACORN was "on the verge of maybe perpetrating one of the greatest frauds in voter history in this country, maybe destroying the fabric of democracy."

The study also examines the manner in which a network of conservative media organizations (the so-called echo chamber) tested and promoted their narrative frames and channeled the stories into mainstream media. The study's authors term the seamlessness of the campaign against ACORN "startling," noting that in 2008 almost everything that the McCain-Palin campaign said about ACORN was exactly what the right-wingers in the media had said themselves. The original campaign, they note, was concocted by conservative politicians upset with ACORN's community organizing efforts to help poor Americans improve economic conditions and gain a stronger political voice. After the election, the authors explain, these same conservatives continued to attack ACORN and tried to link ACORN to Obama and the Democrats. Criticism of ACORN has been a consistent story on Fox News and conservative talk shows and in conservative publications, Web sites, and columns in mainstream newspapers. For example:

- In early 2009 GOP allegations that the Democrats in Congress specifically targeted billions of stimulus funds for ACORN became news stories even though the allegations were not true.
- In July 2009 Representative Darrell Issa (R-CA), the ranking Republican on the House Oversight and Government Reform Committee, released a report, "Is ACORN Intentionally Structured as a Criminal Enterprise?" that repeated many of the allegations that had been made during the 2008 campaign and that had generated media attention.
- On August 11, 2009, the House Judiciary Committee released more than 5,000 pages of White House and Republican National Committee e-mails, along with transcripts of closed-door testimony by former Bush senior adviser and Deputy Chief of Staff Karl Rove, and Harriet Miers, former White House counsel. The documents revealed that Rove played a central role in the firing of David C. Iglesias, the U.S. attorney in New Mexico, for failing to help Republican election prospects by prosecuting alleged instances of voter fraud by ACORN.

Nearly every major news organization reported on the Judiciary Committee's unveiling of the e-mails and transcripts, but none of them, including the *Chicago Tribune, Los Angeles Times, New York Daily News, New York Times, Washington Post,* and *Wall Street Journal* mentioned that Rove had been specifically focused on attacking ACORN for its voter registration efforts in New Mexico and other states, even though ACORN was mentioned frequently as a conservative target in the investigative documents. But should it surprise anyone that one 2009 poll found that 52 percent of Republicans believed that ACORN had stolen the 2008 election for Barack Obama?

THE "RACISM" OF SHIRLEY SHERROD

The ACORN saga may have been a tragedy for its victims, but the now-infamous case of Shirley Sherrod unfolded more like farce. Once again, the Obama administration conspired in its own humiliation. As E. J. Dionne observes, both the mainstream media and the Obama administration "cower[ed] before a right wing that has persistently forced its propaganda to be accepted as news by convincing traditional journalists that 'fairness' require[d] treating extremist rants as 'one side of the story.'" In this episode Sherrod, a longtime employee of the Department of Agriculture, gave a speech to the NAACP about her struggles to overcome the anger and resentment she had once felt toward white people. In the speech she alluded to an episode twenty-four years earlier in which she had initially denied a couple the help to which they were entitled owing to their race and had then reversed herself, rising above her fears to do what was right. In the doctored video of the event that Breitbart peddled to various cable and Internet viewers, however, Sherrod appeared to be bragging about discriminating against a white couple when in fact she was giving personal testimony to just the opposite: She had overcome racism, not embraced it. Fox ran the story without any independent investigation of its own.

Meanwhile, Secretary of Agriculture Tom Vilsack panicked lest his department become the victim of an ACORN-style attack and fired Sherrod without bothering to get to the truth himself. Like the reporters who covered him, Vilsack did not even take the time to watch the entire video in question, despite clear evidence that it had been doctored. (Sherrod later said Deputy Undersecretary Cheryl Cook had demanded her resignation, telling her, "Do it because you're going to be on *Glenn Beck* tonight.") When CNN sought out the elderly husband

and wife who were the alleged victims of the story—the incident in question had actually happened twenty-four years earlier when Sherrod worked the Georgia field office for the Federation of Southern Cooperative/Land Assistance Fund—and learned that she had actually helped them with their loan, rather than the reverse, the administration learned that it had been taken for a fool and was forced to apologize.

At that point Breitbart admitted that, yes, he had engaged in a deliberate (and successful) deception, but his real target had been the NAACP for allegedly cheering on Sherrod's alleged racism. This, too, turned out to be a lie. There was no applause in the undoctored video for any racist statements. Nothing Breitbart had said about the story checked out once the full video became available. And yet this was the man whom reporters and producers trusted so implicitly that they simply ran with his version of events. (And in a not-so-surprising denouement to the original ACORN story, James O'Keefe, Breitbart's star reporter, was arrested by FBI agents in early 2010 together with three associates for attempting an illegal break-in into the offices of Senator Mary Landrieu (D-LA) for the purposes of doctoring her phone lines for another ACORN-like sabotage scheme. He and his friends pled guilty to charges of entering federal property under false pretenses. A few months later in the fall of 2010, he was caught attempting to lure CNN reporter Abbie Boudreau alone onto a boat filled with sex toys, pornographic magazines, a "condom jar," "fuzzy handcuffs," "an obvious sex tape machine," and hidden cameras, where he—rather bizarrely—hoped to film her en flagrante after he had fooled her into who knows what. Fortunately, Boudreau had been tipped off in advance and declined the invitation.)

WHAT LIBERAL MEDIA?

Conservatives complain and complain about alleged liberal domination of the media and yet continue to enjoy kid-glove treatment in their most influential forums. Take a look at the guest lists, for instance, for

the six most influential Sunday news programs for the first sixteen
months of the Obama presidency. According to one careful study, between January 2009 and April 2010 "six Sunday television talk shows
[were] dominated by men, whites and Republicans, particularly right-
wing Republicans, with a geographical bias for the East and Midwest.
This was true of the guests, reporters and pundits." The bias is partially
establishment driven. Bookers and producers demonstrate a weakness
for the safe, predictable, and familiar. "The folks at *Politico* appear multiple times but nobody from TPM. You hear from the Washington
Examiner, but nothing from the Washington Independent." During
this sixteen-month period, "one independent Senator, Joe Lieberman of
Connecticut, made nine appearances, while the other independent,
Bernie Sanders, made a single appearance." The top invitees among
politicians were Republican Mitch McConnell (twenty-five appearances), Republican John McCain (twenty-one), Republican John Kyl
(eighteen), Republican Lindsey Graham (eighteen), and Republican
Mike Huckabee (thirteen), who tied with the top Democrat, Charles
Schumer. Newt Gingrich, who doesn't even have a current position in
government, came in next, with twelve appearances. Among pundits,
Fox's Juan Williams (fifty-six), Bill Kristol (fifty-six), and Mara Liasson
(fifty-one) led the way, followed by ABC's conservative George Will
(forty-four), Brit Hume (twenty-eight), and another Foxite and *New
York Times* conservative David Brooks (twenty). The first liberal to
make it into the mix was the *New York Times*'s Paul Krugman (sixteen).
A similar tilt can be found among the guests on PBS's nightly *Newshour*
broadcast between centrist establishment and firebrand conservative
voices, leaving liberals out in the cold. According to a study published
by Fairness and Accuracy in Reporting, the *Newshour*'s guest list during
a two-month period spanning May and June 2010 contained think
tank sources from right-leaning groups (at least 50 percent). "With just
four sources (13 percent), left-leaning think tanks were outnumbered
by right-leaning ones 4 to 1."

The continued fealty of mainstream institutions to conservatives and the purveyors of Washington conventional wisdom has important consequences for the Obama administration's ability to focus public debate. To give one slight example of why this matters, at the end of 2009, federal officials arrested the so-called underpants bomber en route to the United States, where he sought, with considerable incompetence, to blow up a passenger airliner. Recall that when the so-called shoe bomber got past security in late December 2001, the Bush White House simply clammed up, and the media (and the Democrats) were happy to go along. The president did not mention the shoe bomber at all until a press conference six days after the incident took place. Meanwhile, after the shenanigans of Mr. Underpants, Barack Obama issued three public statements and announced two security reviews and a directive on how to try to correct the problem. So what did we hear? "In the Obama administration, protecting the rights of terrorists has been more important than protecting the lives of Americans," explained Newt Gingrich during one of his frequent appearances on *Meet the Press*. "I don't know that Obama has the same ability to reflect the emotions of the country as Bush did at certain points in his presidency," worried its host, David Gregory. And when, with almost breathtaking lunacy, Rudy Giuliani went on ABC's *Good Morning America* to insist, "We had no domestic attacks under Bush; we've had one under Obama," George Stephanopoulos, the show's host, chose not to subject this rather unusual claim to any additional scrutiny and simply let it pass unchallenged.

Even without the heavy overlay of right-wing propaganda, the American media as they are now constituted would be hard-pressed to provide the kind of information and opportunity for debate required if the president were to undertake fundamental liberal reforms of our various dysfunctional institutions and outdated public policies. It is no secret that, with just a few laudable exceptions, complicated stories about government proposals and their likely implications do not excite what remains of a decimated journalistic establishment. Sensationalism, not substance, is what drives ratings. True, it has ever been thus, but the intensity of this focus has increased enormously in our age of celebrity obsession and the ongoing blurring of news and gossip. At one of President Obama's earliest press conferences, CNN's Ed Henry repeatedly badgered the president, demanding to know why he allowed other politicians—in this case then-Attorney General of New York Andrew Cuomo—to exhibit their anger about AIG's executive bonuses before he had a chance to do so. "So on AIG, why did you wait—why did you wait days to come out and express that outrage? . . . It took you days to come public with Secretary Geithner and say, 'Look, we're outraged.' Why did it take so long?" Obama's answer—"Well, it took us a couple of days because I like to know what I'm talking about before I speak"— did not appear to impress Henry, who actually bragged about this exchange afterward. "From just a few feet away, I could see in his body language that the normally calm and cool president was perturbed," he noted, as if this were somehow the appropriate job description for a White House reporter. Then again, Henry may have had a point, however pathetic, as many of his colleagues appear to share his odd view of what constitutes journalistic responsibility in today's mainstream media. Here, for instance, is an exchange between press secretary Robert Gibbs and CBS's Chip Reid in the briefing room on the president's reaction to the BP oil spill:

REID: I haven't—have we really seen rage from the president on this? I think most people would say no.
GIBS: I've seen rage from him, Chip. I have.
REID: Can you describe it? Does he yell and scream? What does he do?

And remember, this was CBS, not Fox.
Now recall the health care debate, which may have been the most heavily covered political issue of most of our lifetimes. How much of it

focused on the personality conflicts and the political struggles of Pelosi and Reid to cobble together their respective majorities in the face of competing claims, such as, say, between the pro- and the antiabortion senators and representatives? And how much of the coverage focused on the money lobbyists were pouring into the campaigns, or on the fine points of the legislation they were writing, or on the political threats they were making lest the laws be written in an unfavorable fashion? To say "none at all" would be an exaggeration; some coverage was really quite good, but these analyses obviously constituted a tiny percentage of the political news stories of the period, much of which focused on town hall meetings featuring an awful lot of people who forgot to take their meds that day.

Even at the highest levels of the profession, personality trumps substance at every turn. It speaks volumes about the contemporary state of political journalism to note that *Game Change*, John Heilemann and Mark Halperin's best-seller about the 2008 election, offered up the story of John and Elizabeth Edwards's marriage troubles in excruciating detail but said next to nothing about the policy differences that separated the candidates or what such differences might imply for their respective presidencies. Meanwhile, *Politico*, the well-funded and financially successful new publication that increasingly sets the tone for so much insider coverage, displays virtually no interest in policy and instead merely offers up a constant scorecard of who's up, who's down, and who's "driving the convo" that day. As Mark Liebovich notes in his lengthy *New York Times Magazine* profile of *Politico*'s star reporter, Mike Allen, the publication's headline over its coverage of President Obama's health care summit was "No Clear Winner in Seven-Hour Gabfest." Former McCain adviser Mark Salter notes of *Politico*'s widespread influence, "They have taken every worst trend in reporting, every single one of them, and put them on rocket fuel. . . . It's the shortening of the news cycle. It's the trivialization of news. It's the gossipy nature of news. It's the self-promotion."

The relentless trivialization of the news is in part a function of the explosion of news outlets, almost all of which fail to invest in actual reporting and hence spend their time chasing the same set of stories with the same information—only the "personalities" offering the commentary distinguish one from the other. The trend is most pronounced on cable news, but it spreads through the media like an infectious disease. For instance, the nonsensical "Balloon Boy" story of 2009, which turned out to be a silly, publicity-seeking hoax, received 16 percent of all available airtime from October 12 to 18 on the twenty-four-hour cable networks, according to the Pew Center. Afghanistan did not rate even half as much time, despite key battles taking place between the Taliban and regular Pakistani forces on Pakistani soil that very week. Similarly, when Michael Jackson died that June, stories relating to his life and death accounted for fully 36 percent of all cable news airtime; it remained in the top ten stories a month later, though as it happened, Jackson was still dead.

Even when the topic is allegedly serious political news, ridiculousness is the rule. During the 2010 midterm elections, the candidate who received more coverage than any other was Delaware Republican Christine O'Donnell. The onetime antimasturbation crusader who dabbled in witchcraft, never held an actual job, defaulted on both her student loans and her mortgage, and rejected the doctrines of both evolution and separation of church and state won her party's nomination with barely 50,000 votes—barely enough people to fill a football stadium. And yet her good looks and idiotic comments made her the single top story of the election; despite the fact that it should have been obvious to anyone paying attention that she was never going to be a U.S. senator, she received 50 percent more coverage than any other candidate for office, according to the Project on Excellence in Journalism.

Then there's the stupidity. Together with an insouciant lack of concern for evidence, context, or even simple logic that characterizes so much of our right-leaning media, it is a wonder that any sensible liberal argument ever reaches the larger public. For sheer idiocy, it would be hard to top a Fox clip I happened to catch on the *Daily Show* in which Laura Ingraham was seen to argue that the American people supported torture because the ratings for the Fox network's recently canceled program *24* constituted a national referendum on the issue. I swear I am not making this up. This is a woman who, back in the 1990s, was chosen by the *CBS Evening News* to appear alongside Bill Bradley as the network's regular commentator on the news, a role once played by Bill Moyers. And speaking of CBS, Ben Domenech, a former Bush administration aide and Republican Senate staffer, was able to publish on the network's Web site in April 2010 his observation that President Obama would "please" much of his base by picking Elena Kagan as the country's "first openly gay justice." Here Domenech demonstrated perhaps all of the qualities that simultaneously make sensible discussion of complicated political questions in the American media so difficult. First, the young man was lying. Kagan was not "openly gay" and never had been. (As it happens, I had personally reported that Kagan "was not openly gay" just days earlier on the "Daily Beast" in the context of identifying candidates who were. Many others did as well after Stevens announced his impending retirement.) Second, the statement was entirely personal and prurient, having nothing whatever to do with her legal views. Third, CBS, which originally refused to take down the post despite a complete lack of any attempt at verification, offered credibility to this falsehood, further eroding the distinction between this once respected MSM news organization and the most petty, partisan corners of the blogosphere. (Domenech later defended himself by insisting he had heard the claim "mentioned casually on multiple occasions by friends and colleagues.") Fourth, to add insult to injury, this very same blogger had earlier been hired and resigned over a three-day period by a no-less-desperate *Washington Post* after he was discovered to be a serial plagiarist. It was a sad development for the standards of mainstream journalism when the *Post* felt it necessary to hire someone like Domenech in the first place. And here he was again on CBS, playing out the farce.

One would think such irresponsibility on the part of a mainstream media organization would demonstrate the limits of the MSM's willingness to pander to right-wing smear tactics. Sadly, on Election Day 2010, ABC News managed to top even this. It invited, I kid you not, the admitted liar, video-doctor, and sponsor of criminals-who-pretend-to-be-journalists, Andrew Breitbart, to contribute his analysis to its 2010 Election Night coverage. But following an Internet outcry over the incident, ABC apparently changed its collective mind and let Breitbart know that he had been un-invited, according to a letter from the network's Andrew Morse, owing to the "widespread misimpression" his blogging about the event had created. Even though Breitbart was no longer welcome, however, the editor of his "Big Journalism" site, Dana Loesch, was. And so despite the posting of pieces on the site calling ABC "cowardly" and a "wuss," and another arguing that ABC had shown it could be "muscled and intimidated," Loesch got to enjoy the role on the news that night that her boss had been forced to forfeit.

Recall that Breitbart has pronounced himself "committed to the destruction of the old media guard." But there is apparently no limit to the humiliation—up to and including a known liar and news fabricator committed to its destruction on a network's Election Day coverage—to which these once proud media organizations will subject themselves in the hopes of somehow appeasing their conservative critics. And yet here was the prism through which Barack Obama was supposed to communicate the priorities of his administration and hold opponents accountable for the obstacles they put in his way.

CONCLUSION

It's Here They Got the Range and the Machinery for Change*

If America is to ameliorate its current democratic dysfunction any-time soon, then merely electing better candidates to Congress is not going to be enough. We need a system that has fairer rules, that diminishes the role of money, and that encourages politicians and journalists to honestly investigate and portray the realities they actually observe, thereby reducing the distorting lenses of finance, ideology, and ignorance. And yet these items rarely feature on any progressive agenda. This is, in many ways, understandable. Ending the Bush/Cheney administration, and defeating the Christian conservative and corporate base on whose behalf it acted, required emergency measures of a largely defensive nature. And the chance to replace George W. Bush with Barack Hussein Obama—both for symbolic and, in many respects, pragmatic reasons in 2008—appeared so enticing (and exciting) that we can all be forgiven for losing ourselves in the romance of focusing our political time, money, and energies on making this man America's forty-fourth president.

But the fact remains that the 2008 election was not a "game change" after all. For genuine change of the kind Obama promised

---

*Ari Melber, an attorney and a *Nation* contributing writer, researched and drafted the legislative and campaign-finance-reform-related sections of this chapter.

and so many progressives imagined, we need to elect politicians willing to challenge the outdated rules of the Senate, willing to fight for publicly financed elections, and, in the absence of that, willing to struggle against the Supreme Court's insistence on giving corporations the same free speech rights as individuals. We need smarter organizations that pressure politicians as well as pundits and reporters, not necessarily to see things our way, but to hold true to the ideals they profess to represent in the first place. We must work to transform our culture to re-ennoble the notion of the "public good."

None of these tasks are likely to be as simple and easy as electing Barack Obama president of the United States was—though to be fair, none look quite as difficult as did electing a certain African American state senator with a name that rhymed with "Osama" and had "Hussein" in the middle as president just five years. Some necessary changes appear awfully simple—which can easily lead people to confuse them with being easy. Some of the challenges standing in our way are genuinely impossible to overcome, like the blatant limitations on democracy inherent within the Electoral College or a Constitution that grants Wyoming and California the same power in the Senate. Others, meanwhile, are maddeningly complex, such as Senate rules regarding cloture and the like. But particularly in light of the 2010 elections, apathy is no option at all. A little imagination and a great deal of hard work and patience can help put us on a path to a more democratic and equitable America. But don't expect it to be easy, and don't be surprised at the resistance of those who profit from politics-as-usual.

THE BROKEN SENATE

The U.S. Congress has become a place where, most of the time, nothing much happens. Once every great while, however, owing to the political investments of one side or another, some massive piece of transformative legislation grows too big to fail and is somehow rammed through Congress without much concern for exactly the same parliamentary niceties that had—right up until that moment—dominated the process. The Obama administration succeeded in passing health care reform and financial regulation in this fashion but failed with cap and trade.

Most voters do not follow politics particularly closely and hence remain largely uninformed about the precise manner of our system's dysfunction. This allows activists who work on specific issues to manipulate the process and thereby shape legislation right up until the final vote without really much of anyone paying attention. And even though once upon a time partisans were satisfied earning a legislator's "nay" vote, the new expectation has become to find a way to kill it.

Clearly, the secret hold that allows individual senators to delay business on any legislation pretty much for as long as they like deserves to die. The Senate has recently attempted to quash this practice. In a standoff that captures some of the absurdity of this body's present method of self-policing, a 2006 bill to expose secret holds was itself the victim of a series of secret holds. To quote Senator Ron Wyden (D-OR) from the floor debate, "That pretty much says it all." Eventually, the Senate did pass legislation—the Honest Leadership and Open Government Act—that purported to end secret holds and demanded that senators stand by them in public. But, true to form, the act lacked any credible enforcement mechanism. It will likely change nothing at all.

A more effective tack would be to remove the fiction of proxy holds from the Senate rules. New rules might state that any senator who issues an objection on the Senate floor must take public responsibility for the hold by the end of that day's session unless another senator asks to be credited in his stead. This would ensure that any politician listed on a controversial hold could force his colleague to take the political heat for it or withdraw the hold. It is hard to imagine the targets of many recent holds being able to withstand that test.

Bringing all holds out into the open would subject them to public accountability and backlash. But the undemocratic ability of a single senator to stop most Senate business would remain. Apart from the unanimous consent procedure, party leaders generally choose to honor holds as evidence of a senator's credible threat to filibuster (even in cases where it seems obvious that a senator has little intention of making good on the actual threat itself). Countering that gridlock requires addressing the filibuster itself. Although rules surrounding filibusters may be arcane, effective reform need not be. The key objective must be to preserve the legitimate tactic of reasonable delay by a dedicated minority to provide for more debate, more information, and more public awareness about proposals that could soon carry the force of permanent law, while at the same time preventing purposeful and permanent obstruction of majority rule. For example, the Patriot Act, which sailed through Congress in just seven days during the panic after the September 11 attacks, would clearly have been a better law if a group of senators had had the foresight (and political courage) to ensure that its most controversial aspects had been given a more thoughtful and thorough hearing.

One sensible alternative would be to simply reduce, over time, the number of votes required to end a filibuster. Currently, a vote to end a filibuster requires sixty votes. Senator Tom Harkin (D-IA) has proposed a gradual approach to grinding that number down to a simple majority. An opening vote to "break" a filibuster would still require sixty votes, but a second motion following a forty-eight-hour delay might need only fifty-seven votes, and so on. Then the number needed would eventually reach fifty-one. Ultimately, the majority would rule, but the minority would retain the opportunity to delay that victory and draw attention to its concerns in the process.

CORPORATIONS, UNITED

The reforms for these structural constraints, however, are hindered not only by the structural constraints themselves—like the Kafkaesque secret hold on a bill to ban secret holds—but also by the character of the reform constituency. It's not easy to convince incumbents to reform the system from which they have already worked so hard to gain. As *Newsweek* columnist Ezra Klein notes, "They've got donor networks, relationships with lobbyists, corporate friends, and activist groups that will help them. Their challengers don't."

What's more, it can be awfully difficult to get media attention for process and precedent. And it's a rather significant challenge to convert the public disgust with Washington and concerns about corporate corruption of political power into informed support for procedural proposals that operate at least one layer apart from policies that actually affect people's lives. Finally, it is no simple matter to convince good-government liberals concerned with such matters to play the kind of hardball required to actually win the fights these reforms inevitably involve.

The severity of our current political crisis may change some of these dynamics. For example, an unusual alliance of twenty-seven high-dollar donors went "on strike" for the first time in 2010, pledging to withhold donations from candidates unless they supported a public funding system for congressional races. "I'd rather have campaign finance reform than access," explained one of the members, Steve Kirsch, a businessman who says he funneled more than $10 million to back Al Gore in 2000. The effort was organized by Change Congress, a group founded in 2008 by political consultant Joe Trippi and activist/legal scholar Lawrence Lessig. So far the numbers have been tiny compared to the flood of private spending currently swamping our system, which is understandable, as this is an awfully risky strategy to pursue when the other side refuses to play along.

This is always the problem with organizing around secondary or "procedural" issues, and it is not an easy one to solve. What some people like to call "acting on principle" others might just as sensibly deem showing up for a gunfight with an iPad. Some low-dollar donors on ActBlue, the largest liberal portal for online campaign contributions, are giving contributions to candidates who back reform. Blue America, a fund-raising network that raised more than $500,000 for liberal candidates, has begun using support for the Fair Elections bill as a criterion for its endorsements. So even though public opinion overwhelmingly favors cleaning up Washington, these insider financial efforts are also crucial for paving an inside track toward reform, albeit slowly, cautiously, and with decidedly mixed results.

Perhaps more promising was a strategy unveiled immediately after the 2010 election when a group of twenty-five investors announced the filing of shareholder resolutions at several corporations that sit on the board of the U.S. Chamber of Commerce, demanding that these boards review their policies and oversight of political expenditures, especially through trade associations, given the organization's aggressive and partisan use of its funds during the midterm election as well as its role in helping to defeat the passage of Obama's cap-and-trade legislation. The first four companies to receive this resolution are Accenture, IBM, Pepsi, and Pfizer, with AT&T, Caremark, Caterpillar, Deere & Company, Dow Chemical, FedEx, JPMorgan Chase & Co., UPS, and Xerox soon to follow. Shareholder democracy is one of the most underutilized tools of political advocacy—at least by those on the left—and hence one with among the most significant potential for genuine action in a moment when the courts have so weakened any remaining strictures on corporate spending.

It is perhaps not so surprising that the problem of political reform in the Senate comes down to the power of the purse, one that the U.S. Supreme Court has greatly exacerbated in recent years with its corporate-friendly rulings in virtually all matters relating to money and speech. The most practical way to combat private financial influence in campaign funding is to reduce it. Yet so long as the Supreme Court continues to equate money with speech and corporations with people, legalized bribery is likely to continue corrupting the system.

Absent an awaking upon the part of a majority of Supreme Court justices, the only practical avenue to empowering the public interest in these battles is to subsidize candidates in the cost of their campaigns. In this model—a public funding system—competing candidates agree to cap their spending in exchange for government funding. The cost of campaigning drops, and the amount of money that candidates accept from private donors is drastically reduced. And even though participation is voluntary, candidates are often eager to embrace it. How much more enjoyable—to say nothing of convenient—it would be for candidates to cash a campaign check for a few million dollars rather than endlessly work the phones begging rich folks for money.

Public funding is an elegant remedy to the problem of institutional corruption: Instead of accepting legal bribes from donors in exchange for special consideration for contributors, candidates receive money from taxpayers in exchange for a pledge to spend less on their campaigns. And it works. Without much fanfare, public funding operated effectively for six consecutive elections, beginning in 1976, when candidates in both parties accepted funds in exchange for spending limits. The campaigns were cheaper, candidates spent less time with a tin cup in their hands, and both parties enjoyed relative financial parity. The parties split elections four to three during that period, and challengers beat incumbents in three out of the five races when incumbent presidents ran for reelection.

One obvious problem with the model, however, is that it leaves one side or the other at a clear disadvantage if it decides to opt in and the other side does not, as happened to John McCain in 2008. Moreover, even when Congress did pass the moderate McCain-Feingold legislation in 2002, since decimated by the U.S. Supreme Court, it failed to pass the component of the bill that was designed to rationalize the cost of campaigns: a limit on what broadcast and television stations could charge for campaign commercials. The provision in question, originally passed by the Senate by a 69 to 31 margin, died in

the House of Representatives following a furious lobbying campaign
by the National Association of Broadcasters and the cable television
industry, leaving the United States alone among 146 countries, according to one study, in refusing to provide free television time to political
candidates. As a result, more money is now needed in the system to
offset the recent explosion of private funding as well as the rising costs
of American political campaigns.

But presidential elections are not the main problem. Congress is.
And its members have traditionally proven quite adept at protecting
their prerogatives, particularly when it comes to retaining their jobs.
The House and Senate have taken a range of small steps to regulate
campaigns in recent years. They agreed to ban companies and unions
from directly contributing to candidates, capped the amount that individual citizens can give, limited the use of "soft money" by the political
parties, and regulated how independent groups spend money on television commercials. Even though these restrictions have some impact
on the margins of a few elections, they are far from the main event.
The truth is that, even though Congress supports public funding for
presidential campaigns, it continues to resist it for itself. This is understandable. On Capitol Hill incumbents typically enjoy a consistent
fund-raising advantage over their challengers, and they like it that way.
As the late Senator Robert Byrd (D-WV) declared in 1987, "The need
for congressional campaign financing reform is obvious, but just because it is obvious does not mean that it is easy to attain."

Yet the times may be a-changing, if only for reasons of self-
interest. Former Republican senator from Maine William Cohen
told Charlie Rose in August 2010 that he found the pressure put on
candidates for Congress by lobbyists to be "obscene," adding, "If the
American people saw what legislators go through, [with lobbyists
saying,] 'Don't forget we supported you in your campaign,' I think
the American public would finally turn against that." And this disgust is not confined to former officials and outsiders. Newer,

younger members increasingly say the process is both miserable and untenable. In a 2010 survey of freshman members, *Politico* found congressional schedules packed with several hours of fund-raising per day. That includes hours of "call time"—phone-banking potential donors from the "cramped cubicles" of campaign committee offices that one freshman likened to a "sweatshop."

The above is true at pretty much every level of politics. Retiring Democratic senator from Indiana Evan Bayh told *Newsweek* on the eve of his retirement, "It's miserable. . . . It is not uncommon to have a fundraiser for breakfast, for lunch, and for dinner, and if you have spare time in between, you go to an office off Capitol Hill and you dial for dollars. Then the weekend rolls around, and you get on a plane and travel the countryside with a tin cup in your hand. And it gets worse each cycle." What's more, in the most critical cases the majority of the money does not even come from within the states. In Democrat John Kerry's 2008 Massachusetts Senate race, for example, two-thirds of both candidates' contributions were from out of state. Consider the absurdity: Wealthy donors who cannot legally vote on the outcome of a local representative election because the winner will not represent them can wield far more influence at the ATM than at the ballot box. Tea Party activists who managed to get themselves so excited about alleged violations of the Constitution by liberal Democrats might wish to take a moment to consider the inherent abrogation of the Founders' intent by this blatant practice of people who have no standing as voters buying elections. Then again we might wait an entire lifetime for such an awakening. In the meantime, plenty remains to be done.

Again, the clearest path to fixing this mess is voluntary public funding. The Fair Elections Now Act, which enjoys more than 140 cosponsors, would create a public funding system for Congress modeled after the presidential system administered by the Federal Elections Commission. The act would allow candidates to collect

$100 donations (or less) from residents of their own states, which would then be matched four to one with Fair Elections funds. Fair Elections would be funded by the sale of unused broadcast spectrum and hence would not pass along any costs to taxpayers at all. This would dramatically reduce the overall spending in a host of races where outside donors dominate the process. That alone would open up elections to candidates unable or unwilling to sell themselves to big funders. Moreover, it would nudge candidate fund-raising back into the business of actual representation, which was, after all, the original intention of the Constitution when the bodies were created. That the act made it through the Committee on House Administration in late September 2010 was a welcome and somewhat surprising development, but it is a long way from a Rose Garden signing ceremony.

A different potential tack, suggested to me by President Richard Trumka of the AFL–CIO, would be to accept that corporate campaign spending, defined as free speech by the U.S. Supreme Court, is a lost battle and focus instead on redefining the meaning of the term "corporation." Trumka suggests that those companies that wish to enjoy all of the benefits of the law, such as limited liability and privileged tax status, agree not to engage in political agitation. Those that do choose to play politics will continue to have every right to do so but will be forced to forfeit all of the protections that incorporation has so far implied. This reform is possible because states determine the various rules and regulations of those corporations whose charters are located in the states. The obvious problem with the notion is that it would require all fifty states to act as one because any single state could tie up the entire system, but it is at least indicative of innovative thinking about what have in the past appeared to be insurmountable obstacles.

A glaring conflict of interest noted earlier, both for members of Congress and for their staffs, is the tempting prospect of quadrupling their salary with a job after government service as long as they keep these potential employers happy. President Obama did keep his campaign pledge and formally banned most lobbyists from working in his administration. That rule acknowledged the revolving door between government and industry, but it stopped people only on the way into government and only within the executive branch. The rule did nothing to address Congress, where the real horse trading takes place. After all, the problem is less whether lobbyists come to work in government, where pay is lower, hours longer, and financial disclosure forms far more onerous, and more whether people leave government to cash in on their connections (and sometimes even to be paid off for services rendered). When the top staffer for the House Banking Committee jumps ship for Goldman Sachs in the middle of a big fight over the regulation of Goldman itself—and can do so without violating any regulations of his federal employment—old-fashioned cash in an envelope becomes unnecessary.

Until 2007 federal law required government officials to wait just one year before taking jobs lobbying their former colleagues. When Congress extended the break to two years and applied the law to a wider circle of congressional staff and administration officials, it drove one senator into early retirement. Senator Trent Lott from Mississippi, a former Republican majority leader, quit, Sarah Palin–style, before his term was up just to ensure that he could cash in on his old job without bothering to wait an extra year. The new regulation was a start. Yet the goal cannot be simply to inconvenience the future Trent Lotts of the world. It must be to root out the encouragement that the current system offers to staffers to sell themselves to the highest bidder.

But again, how? We need a lobbying ban to insulate our elected officials and their top staffers from the temptation to sell themselves to the highest bidder while doing the people's business—and for a few years afterward. In business terms ex-officials and their staff members need to be forced to protect their trade secrets and lay down robust noncompete clauses. A strong ban on employment with firms doing business under legislation covered by the elected officials and relevant staffers would need to run from eight to twelve years. In 2010 Senator Michael Bennet (D-CO) introduced the Closing the Revolving Door Act, which would extend the ban on congressional staff to six years and proposed a lifetime ban on members of Congress from becoming lobbyists after they retire. Passage of this bill, which was referred to the Committee on Homeland Security and Governmental Affairs and at this writing remains stuck there, would restore some independence to government staffers and lawmakers as it simultaneously reduces the stack of chips with which corporate lobbyists arrive at the legislative poker table. But given the turnover in government, even a break that spanned two or three presidential terms and five to seven congressional sessions would ensure that public servants who turn to lobbying later in life would be trading on general knowledge of government, which is legitimate, as opposed to merely exploiting their personal relationships and inside information for those who could afford to pay for it.

A HOUSE DIVIDED . . .

But let's be honest: Any sustained pressure on our politicians is going to require more pressure—and better organization—than progressives have been able to muster since the Obama administration came to power. A big part of the problems that progressives face today is attributable to genuine political weakness. The right is wealthier than the left. No surprise there, as Republicans are, after all, the party of capital. But they are also far better organized and, sad to say, self-disciplined in their ability to act in concert to pressure politicians to achieve their goals, as successful political movements have traditionally been able to do. As journalist Harold Meyerson rightly observes, thinking of both the New Deal and the civil rights reforms of Lyndon Johnson's Great Society, "In America, major liberal reforms require not just liberal governments, but autonomous, vibrant mass movements,

usually led by activists who stand at or beyond liberalism's left fringe."
Indeed, "Both FDR and LBJ had to respond to large and potent insur-
gencies on their left—industrial labor for Roosevelt, black freedom for
Johnson," adds historian Michael Kazin. "Each of these movements
had gestated for decades before emerging as a force that could make or
unmake a presidency." Today, liberals and progressives have nothing
remotely comparable.

In many respects, it might be considered a historical oddity that
the left has had so little success in rallying its supporters into a vibrant
political movement, particularly when the right has managed to organize on exactly the same issues that one might have expected to have
galvanized the left. Take, for instance, the gouging of the middle class.
During the 2000s, with a conservative Republican in the presidency
and a mostly Republican Congress, the inflation-adjusted income of
the median household fell 4.8 percent between 2000 and 2009, even
worse than the 1970s, when median income rose 1.9 percent despite
high unemployment and inflation. Between 2007 and 2009, incomes
fell 4.2 percent. This is of a piece with the flat-to-negative growth of
most wage-earning family incomes ever since the early 1970s. And yet
since 1979, the top 1 percent of Americans have enjoyed 36 percent
of all the gains made in household wealth (and this includes government benefits). Between 2001 and 2006, their share of income gains
was an amazing 53 percent. Even more amazing, perhaps, is the fact
that between 1979 and 2005, the top 0.1 percent—or one out of
every one thousand households—took home 20 percent of all income
gains (after taxes). Think about it. Approximately 300,000 superrich
Americans gobbled up half again as much of the fruits of new wealth
produced as 180 million or so American workers. Just over thirty
years ago, CEOs of Fortune 500 companies earned, on average, forty-
two times what the average American worker did and about 9 percent
of the nation's annual income. Today, they make, on average, 531
times what their remaining workers take home and gobble up nearly

24 percent of the nation's income. This explosion of inequality threatens the fundamental functioning of democracy. It can hardly be a coincidence that it has come at a time when the labor movement has been fighting off a thirty-year war by corporate America, with labor's power and influence over the private economy dwindling, while the right has benefited from the introduction into the system of a veritable flood of corporate cash. After the 2008 election, many activists had great hopes for movement-building measures by the Obama administration to continue throughout his presidency. Instead, we got the Tea Party.

Clearly, liberals and progressives must pay more attention to the need to strengthen organized labor, which, together with (once) progressive churches and synagogues, has traditionally provided perhaps the most powerful voice and the armies for pretty much all successful progressive movements for the past century. We desperately need an expanded political agenda that includes investing in the kind of jobs and education needed to train our workforce to compete with a globalized workforce, oftentimes in places where wages are low and labor and environmental enforcement is lax to nonexistent. Working closely with labor to address the challenges of global competition and of the assault on the rights of workers and the laws that had previously protected them has to be a priority of any potentially successful progressive movement in the United States.

So, too, does an embrace of legal immigration in America. As John Judis and Ruy Teixeira predicted back in 2004, an "emerging Democratic majority" was on the rise owing in significant measure to the increasing Hispanicization of much of the nation and that rise would continue so long as progressives were able to earn the trust of these new citizens, as the party had done with new immigrants during the late nineteenth and early twentieth centuries. The xenophobic hysterics currently on display at Tea Party rallies and among right-wing cable talk show and talk radio hosts have forced Republican Party politicians, such as John McCain (AZ), who once supported a relatively generous policy of immigration reform, to repudiate their former selves in exchange for an angry rhetorical stance that scapegoats immigrants. This quite obviously offers liberals an opportunity, indeed an almost open field. Barack Obama's 67 percent of the Hispanic vote in 2008 should have cemented these gains. But given the complete lack of progress on immigration reform in Congress, coupled with a tendency on the part of Democrats to fear the consequences of openly embracing a path toward legalization for America's 11 or so million undocumented workers, it hasn't worked out that way. (Senate Majority Leader Harry Reid's statement "I don't know how anyone of Hispanic heritage could be a Republican, OK . . . " "Do I need to say more?" appeared to be the sum total of the Democrats' strategy on outreach to these crucially important citizens and potential citizens during the first two years of Obama's presidency.)

The difficulty lies in bringing such groups together. Labor and immigrant groups have traditionally had trouble even communicating with one another because so many native-born workers have themselves blamed immigration for keeping wages artificially low by supplying a pool of nonunionized workers to replace those who threaten to go on strike. Most labor leaders know they have no choice but to embrace these new immigrants, and, indeed, those groups that have are often the only private-sector unions to see their memberships grow in recent decades. Indeed, in the midst of what were unarguably disastrous electoral results for the Democrats in the 2010 midterm elections, one bright spot emerged in California, Arizona, and much of the Southwest, where the labor/immigrant alliance is perhaps at its most advanced and where Spanish-speaking union leaders built an all-but impregnable firewall in defense of the gains they had built over the course of decades of cooperation. It proved a heartening reminder that even though nativist know-nothingism will always be with us and will occasionally explode in moments of economic stress, many Americans are the sons, daughters, grandsons, granddaughters, or even grandparents of immigrants themselves and understand the vital role immigration plays in renewing America's cultural and economic dynamism.

But with so many would-be workers unemployed, coupled with the right's ability to exploit native resentment around the question of immigration, forging alliances has been slow of late. In recent years labor and immigration leaders have collaborated on policies that combine a path toward legal immigration with job training for natural-born Americans so that immigration does not become just a safety valve for large corporations to keep wages artificially depressed for all parties. Indeed, work itself can and should be viewed as a path to Americanization both for recent immigrants and for their children. Liberals need not oppose strict enforcement of the law. The current situation, which has resulted in an estimated 11 million undocumented workers in America today—down from 12 million two years ago—invites exploitation of powerless people and breeds contempt for the law at all levels. What is clearly needed is a path to citizenship for those workers already here as well as rationalization of an out-of-control system that will radically reduce the number of workers here without proper documentation (and therefore legal protection). As a political matter, honest work is the best way to prove to the rest of the nation that they can be valuable allies in the struggle to build a fairer and more (widely) prosperous society. Labor and immigration movement leaders understand that they must work together in the abstract, but the reality has proved more challenging.

Much the same can be said about the labor movement's conflict with the environmental movement. "Green jobs" are, again, the obvious path to future prosperity, but the temporary and painful dislocation caused by the transition to these industries has so far allowed corporate America, together with know-nothing politicians, to exploit the current jobs crisis to undermine crucial environmental initiatives. Investing in green jobs is quite clearly a win-win for the country and the world, but the inability of our political class to see beyond the strictures of deficit-obsessed "fiscal responsibility" has kept off the table the kind of green public works program that might help solve both the jobs and the environmental crises. This, too, represents another failure both of imagination and communication on the part of liberals and progressives.

Finally, there remain historic conflicts between blacks and Hispanics, blacks and Jews, Jews and Arab Americans, urban and rural voters, and so on. Just about everywhere among America's key constituencies, potential conflicts—real and imagined—loom large. These divisions have historically enabled conservatives and corporations to adopt a "divide-and-rule" strategy toward progressives, and, sadly, it has been awfully effective. As any political consultant will be happy to explain, it is far easier to frighten citizens to vote their angst and anger than to embolden them to vote their hopes and dreams. This, together with the relentless propaganda machine of the nativist, right-wing media and the apathy of the mainstream media, is the challenge facing anyone who seeks to organize a movement to oppose the forces described previously. For any hope of success at all, we must rise above these challenges, however difficult it may be.

DON'T MOURN: ORGANIZE

And we must do so, alas, on our own. The Obama administration—in decided contrast to the Obama campaign—has tended to treat the question of movement organizing with kid gloves. David Plouffe, the campaign's top organizer, created an e-mail list of more than 13 million names for future use. Many organizers salivated at the prospect of using that list to build up organizations in support of environmental, economic, and various social causes to mirror the progressive agenda. Even if only 10 percent were diehard progressives willing to give of their time, a movement of 1.3 million members actively seeking "change" throughout the political system appeared to have the potential to effect real political transformation. Plouffe, who took the year after the election off to write a memoir and spend time with his young children after a grueling campaign, appeared in this memoir to embrace the underlying logic of allowing grass roots to grow organically. In *The Audacity to Win*, he wrote of his realization that he had "initially pursued rallies to maintain the perception of the campaign as grass-roots driven," so that the campaign would not appear to be the captive of its big money donors. Eventually, however, the campaign came to treat "citizen fundraisers as no less important than our larger raisers. . . . They believed their effort was valued—and it was—so they dug deeper and kept raising. This was not a tactical relationship. It was authentic. And that authenticity became a very powerful driver in the connection between Barack Obama and his supporters." Too bad this entire effort pretty much came to a halt on Election Day.

Despite the desire of hundreds of thousands of Obama volunteers to continue their efforts on behalf of the administration, according to an online survey conducted by Organizing for America (OFA, the successor organization to Obama for America) the administration was not really interested in promoting any alternative structure to the Democratic Party. The concern most likely was the danger that OFA might develop its own priorities and interfere with those of the administration. (And the Obama administration certainly did not want to encourage primary challenges to sitting Democratic senators. In fact, it went to great lengths in Arkansas, New York, and Pennsylvania to discourage such challenges almost irrespective of the politics of the incumbent in question.) OFA continues to raise money and send out e-mails, but it does not ask for any sustained involvement or even discussion of the issues the administration chooses to address. As Charles Homans observed in the *Washington Monthly*, OFA "looks less like a movement than a cheering section." Meanwhile, the independent organizations that might have arisen with direct, grassroots connections to the concerns of the millions of people who committed themselves to the Obama campaign never arose. The energies and enthusiasm of so many people, including particularly so many young people new to the political process, simply evaporated into the ether, and a historic opportunity to rejuvenate American politics for a generation was lost.

Because the Obama administration is clearly happier with a top-down approach, progressives who take movement organizing seriously need to develop their institutions independently. To do so, however, they will have to put aside traditional differences that have separated them in the past, particularly those between liberals and progressives who think of themselves as left of liberal. MoveOn.org's role has proven exemplary in the past in joining these two groups together and provides a model for future political organization. As Jim Vopat reported in *In These Times*, in Michigan a group of progressives who met through MoveOn house parties established Harbor Country Progress, an official Democratic Party club that helped to transform the political landscape in the state's rural Sixth Congressional District. As G. William Domoff notes in the same publication, replicating this model across the country "allows activists to maintain their primary social and political identities while at the same time enabling them to compete within the Democratic Party." They could be as progressive as they like so long as the campaign stayed positive; and win or lose, everyone would agree to support the Democrat in the election. By working within the current structure to transform the Democratic Party from within, these smart and savvy activists are adopting an alternative to the spoiler strategy adopted by Ralph Nader and his supporters in 2000, which had the effect of helping to hand the presidency to George W. Bush. Also unlike Nader's catastrophic presidential campaigns, this constructive model of transformation evinces the potential to build for the future, particularly one where Internet fund-raising invites the left to compete with the financial power of corporations as never before.

VOTING RIGHTS AND ELECTIONS

Another item on the long-term reform agenda needs to be the question of democracy itself. U.S. politics, with its anemic participation rates, invites too much influence for too many undemocratic forces in our elections. As the American Enterprise Institute's Norman Ornstein noted in response to an earlier version of this argument, to counter the oversized power of such minority interests, "in Australia, where failure to show up at the polls (you can vote for 'none of the above') leads to a $15 fine, attendance is over 95 percent—and politicians cater less to consultants and the extremes (since both bases turn out in equal proportions) and more to the small number of persuadable voters who are not swayed by outrageous rhetoric." A few right-wing libertarians might cry "totalitarianism," but most Americans would likely see it as a reasonable way to ensure that everybody gets their say. After all, nobody's being forced to vote "for anyone," just to affirm their bona fides as small "d" democrats as an essential component of citizenship.

The short-term problem with mandatory voting, however, lies not in its demands on lazy individuals but in the inability of localities to locate and register voters who are legally entitled to vote and identify those who are not. Australia, as it happens, puts most of the onus to register voters on election authorities. Australian election officials gather information from government agencies to identify voting-eligible individuals who are unregistered and then mail these individuals the requisite voting materials. In this respect Australia is not unusual; the United States is. For example, according to one survey of sixteen nations and four Canadian provinces, only four place the onus of voter registration entirely on the individual as the United States does, which helps account for this country's anemic rates of political participation. So, too, as many have pointed out, does our unwillingness to allow people to vote on a weekend or a holiday, when they are not forced to miss work or to wait in line for hours and hours merely to exercise their constitutional right to pick their leaders. (It is almost as if some politicians do not want people—particularly wage workers—to be able to vote.)

As a step from here to there, the Brennan Center for Legal Justice has proposed a program of modernization of current U.S. voter registration practices that, if properly implemented, might increase the number of voters by as many as 65 million people. The plan would remove the onus of voter registration from citizens by placing the responsibility for maintaining voter registration with state governments, which would thereby eliminate the burden of last-minute registration placed on election officials and remove the need for third-party registration drives. By bringing the registration system into the twenty-first century, the plan would eliminate unnecessary bureaucratic processes, save states money, free up precious resources for election officials, and simplify the process for voters. It would further make such registration automatic and permanent, bringing all eligible, unregistered voters onto the rolls and keeping them there even after they move. This is particularly important for members of the military, their families, students, and, of course, the millions of victims of the current foreclosure crisis, many of whom presently lack a permanent address. Some states have already begun to adopt aspects of this program, but making it part of the progressive agenda would likely do wonders for a whole host of related priorities, particularly given the unrestrained spending by corporations and other interested parties in the wake of *Citizens United*.

And a final item on this agenda for expanded and improved democracy needs to be the extension of the right to vote to ex-felons. Millions of Americans have had their right to vote revoked for periods ranging from the time spent incarcerated to a lifetime. In ten states a person can lose the right to vote for life. This is morally indefensible. The right to vote in the United States is not contingent on good behavior any more than it is on race, religion, or ethnicity. And the idea that even after one has paid one's proverbial "debt to society," one must continue to pay with one's right to vote makes no moral or political sense. Most of these laws are rooted in the Jim Crow era and were intended to bar minorities from voting, and many continue to operate that way, with black and Latino voters, particularly males, discouraged or prevented from voting in numbers well beyond their proportional representation in the population. What's more, as in the case of Florida in 2000, confusion regarding differing state felony disfranchisement laws can easily result in eligible voters, sometimes even those with no disqualifying criminal conviction, being purged from the rolls or denied the ability to register to vote or cast their ballots. The provisions of the Democracy Restoration Act, introduced in Congress in July 2009 by Senator Russ Feingold (D-WI) and Representative John Conyers (D-MI), would restore voting rights in federal elections to nearly 4 million Americans who have been released from prison and are living in the community while also ensuring that people on probation would not lose their right to vote in federal elections. This bill deserves the energetic support of all liberals and progressives as a matter of both fairness and strategy. Throughout our history, a more democratic America has consistently helped create a more progressive America, and these steps taken in support of improving democracy will likely help offset other, more reactionary developments recently introduced by the Roberts Court.

THE PROBLEM OF MEDIA: RESCUE AND REFORM

If money is the "mother's milk" of politics, then media must be its baby food. To some conservatives, the media are just another way to make money. Television was "just another household appliance, a toaster with a picture," as Ronald Reagan's appointed head of the Federal Communications Commission, Mark Fowler, famously described it. More ideologically inclined right-wingers have used media as a means of movement building, one that liberals have sought to emulate. But liberals and progressives see another side of media as well. A genuinely diverse and democratic media based in communities of both concern and geography have the power to inform people of facts and evidence and to enable them to form a powerful public voice to stand up to monied and other powerful interests. John Dewey and Walter Lippmann disagreed on a great deal in their famous debate over the value and purpose of media in the formation of "public opinion" during the 1920s, but neither one doubted their importance in terms of giving everyday people the opportunity both to track the actions of their leaders and to form their own views on issues in conjunction with the other members of their communities, however defined.

This view of the media as the essential battlefield in the war of ideas does not diminish their fundamental democratic role as purveyors of honest, nonpartisan information, but it does complicate the means by which that field is approached. Liberals and progressives need to keep up the pressure they have begun to place on the mainstream media not to adopt the deliberately misleading and frequently false frames foisted on readers and viewers by an increasingly self-confident and well-funded right-wing noise machine. Media Matters, FAIR, and other organizations have done this in the past, but they need help. And in an age of instant personal communication—to say nothing of the power of YouTube—there's no reason they can't get it. (This pressure also, and this is key, needs to be polite. No journalist is going to respond to the kind of personal abuse that is all too common in newspaper comment sections and other such forums for MSM complaint.) Done properly, such pressure is an effective means of forcing journalists to rethink some of their reflective prejudices, particularly in today's punishing economic environment. But if progressives continue to pressure the media to live up to the promises of their profession—to refuse to cater to the lowest common denominator of tabloids or the right-wing cesspool of talk radio/cable television discourse—this should strengthen reporters' and editors' backbones to do the kind of the work that made them proud to be journalists in the first place. (This is, happily, a fundamental difference between right- and left-wing media criticism. The right seeks to undermine the messengers of news that does not comport with its worldview; the left wants journalism to stick to its guns and resist such pressures to color the news, believing, as Stephen Colbert once said, that the facts "have a well-known liberal bias.") And on the positive side, we need to support, whether with subscriptions, clicks, or direct donations, those journalistic enterprises and experiments that attempt to live up to their values as it becomes harder and harder to do so.

Groups like Free Press, the Media Access Project, the Center for American Progress, and the New America Foundation, together with Moveon.org, have already done a good job of helping to publicize— and organize—on behalf of issues related to keeping our media open for democratic communication, particularly with regard to media concentration. The danger today, however, is that with the issues growing so complicated, and with media companies encountering difficulties in retaining their commitment to expensive forms of journalism at a time when the advertising base to support such forms is disappearing into the ether, questions relating to the fairness and openness of America's "marketplace of ideas" will be buried beneath an avalanche of both jargon and apathy. Progressives cannot afford to allow this to happen. Though a few foundations and university-affiliated journalism schools have made tentative contributions to filling in what were once the functions of for-profit journalism institutions, more foundations and universities need to be encouraged to step into this breach as well and to do so quickly. As a professor of journalism, I can tell you we are already losing many of our future Seymour Hershes and Jane Mayers to career paths that do not appear to be evaporating before our eyes; indeed, we are losing an entire generation of them. Already, the ratio of public relations people to working journalists is close to four to one; only thirty years ago it was just a little more than one to one. And if you believe you are getting better, more dependable information from PR hacks than from professional journalists, I have a bridge in Brooklyn I'd like to sell you.

Meanwhile, authors Leonard Downie and Michael Schudson report, "Fewer journalists are reporting less news in fewer pages." According to the *State of the News Media* 2010 report, "Newsrooms have shrunk by 25% in [just] the past three years." Those that remain are now called upon to do more and more with less and less: Podcasts, videochats, blogging, and interactive engagement with readers, viewers, and listeners in comments sections all detract from the essential mission of investigation, interpretation, and synthesis for the purposes of informing and educating the larger public. And even though some of these developments have undoubtedly been valuable in forcing an often arrogant and disconnected media establishment to respond to the everyday reality of Americans' actual lives, the overall effect is a diminution in the foundation of public knowledge, the essential foundation of democracy.

A few highly motivated individuals and organizations have attempted to step into the breach by founding new nonprofit media organizations. These include the investigative team of reporters created by Propublica (funded by civic-minded billionaires Herb and Marion Sandler and headed by Paul E. Steiger, former managing editor of the *Wall Street Journal*); the Center for Independent Media, headed by David Bennahum, a former writer at *Wired*; the creation of series of local-news-oriented partnerships with journalism schools, like those at Columbia and the City University of New York (CUNY), that employ faculty and students to cover stories that are no longer economically affordable for local newspapers; and too many other small and still incipient ventures to mention. But however valuable any of these individual efforts turn out to be, they function pretty much like cocktail umbrellas in the midst of a hurricane. With the core news function of for-profit media increasingly on life support in the United States, we need to find ways to preserve investigative journalism and well-informed discourse as a public good, just like public safety and clean air, lest we be left with what Michael J. Copps, a visionary commissioner of the Federal Communications Commission (FCC), describes as "a seriously dumbed-down democratic dialogue, diminished civic engagement and the absence of meaningful public interest oversight."

The airwaves, believe it or not, are owned by the public, not the corporations that profit from them. And yet media companies are able to reap billions from their use of the airwaves with nothing but a "postcard" process of renewal every eight years to determine whether they are even pretending to serve the public interest. A campaign for taxpayer-funded high-quality journalism on the model of the British Broadcasting Corporation (BBC)—and recently suggested by the Downie/Schudson study published by the Columbia University School of Journalism—should not be off the table. Americans currently pay about $1.35 each in tax dollars to support noncommercial media, compared to about $25 in Canada, Australia, and Germany; nearly $60 in Japan; $80 in Britain; and more than $100 in Denmark and Finland. A similar fee in the United States would yield as much a $35 billion every year.

And the proof is in the pudding. If we compare the resources and the potential for intelligent, informative democratic debate between, say, the BBC and our own underfunded, politically cautious Corporation for Public Broadcasting, which funds the Public Broadcasting Service (PBS), it is not a pretty picture. (The loss, for instance, of Bill Moyers on PBS—whose frequently fearless discussions and debates were always a source of decided discomfort to the comfortable coalition of corporate and political players who expect to dominate the news— appears to have left an irreplaceable gap in our broadcast media landscape, despite the commitment of many on PBS and National Public

Radio to do what they can to uphold professional standards of honesty and decency.) As the report's authors argue, "Public radio and television should be substantially reoriented to provide significant local news reporting in every community served by public stations and their Web sites. This requires urgent action by and reform of the Corporation for Public Broadcasting, increased congressional funding and support for public media news reporting, and changes in mission and leadership for many public stations across the country." In particular, they add, "a national Fund for Local News should be created with money the Federal Communications Commission now collects from or could impose on telecom users, television and radio broadcast licensees, or Internet service providers and which would be administered in open competition through state Local News Fund Councils."

Many in the media in particular, but also in private industry, are understandably skeptical, even hostile to anything that smacks of government funding of media, fearing its association with totalitarian regimes and susceptibility to political pressure. But as University of Illinois professor and tireless crusader for media democracy Robert McChesney points out:

> According to the annual ranking of The Economist magazine, those countries with the largest public media and press subsidies are the freest and most democratic nations in the world, ahead of the United States. According to Freedom House, those nations with the largest government press subsidies also have the most flourishing and uncensored private news media, again far ahead of the United States. Indeed, recent research demonstrates that as press subsidies have increased in European nations, the content of the news has become more adversarial toward the party in power and the government in general.

Government funding of media can be done because it is being done, and McChesney and others have come up with citizen-directed schemes to allocate the funds without much (or any) official interference.

An equally significant debate for progressives that is already upon us is the need for the public to enjoy full and unprejudiced access to broadband, wireless communications, and other Internet delivery systems, as do the big media behemoths. The birth of the liberal blogosphere, with its ability to bypass the big media institutions and conduct conversations within a like-minded community, has been an undeniable boon to the notion of a genuinely democratic discourse. The Web provides a powerful platform that enables the creation of communities; distribution is frictionless, swift, and cheap. The old democratic model was a nation of New England towns filled with well-meaning, well-informed yeoman farmers. Thanks to the Web, we can all join in the debate.

Issues such as net neutrality need to be protected against schemes like that put forth recently by Verizon and Google to prioritize the communications of those with money and power and to denude the FCC of any meaningful oversight and regulatory role. Given the importance of these new communications technologies to democratic communication between groups and individuals and the key role of the blogosphere in holding larger media corporations accountable to higher standards of truth and fairness than they would otherwise embrace on their own, the importance of waging this particular fight is difficult to overstate. As Dewey argued in response to Lippmann, the foundation of democracy is not merely information but also conversation. Members of a democratic society need to cultivate what journalism scholar James W. Carey, in describing the debate, called "certain vital habits" of democracy—the ability to discuss, deliberate on, and debate various perspectives in a manner that would move the public toward consensus. Elites and the public are not always in concert either in views and interests. "A class of experts is inevitably so removed from common interests as to become a class with private interests and private knowledge," Dewey argued. It is not enough for us to have merely theoretical "access" to digital communication. The true democratic challenge is for voices to be heard, which is another matter entirely. As Commissioner Copps explained at an August 2010 public hearing on the future of the Internet, "We have a technology now with more power to bring about good than any communications advancement in all of history. The question is: will we use it in such a way as to maximize its small 'd' democratic potential."

Despite the countless complications involved in preserving the independence and integrity of the news while simultaneously setting up fair and unbiased funding mechanisms, ensuring access to broadband communications for everyone, and enabling those without the support of megacorporations to be heard in the public sphere, a strong, vibrant media sector is essential. Without it, the future of informed democratic debate in the United States, public education on crucial issues, and grassroots organizing for citizen action are in jeopardy. For as Walter Lippmann warned almost a century ago, "When the audience is deprived of independent access to information," the public is left at the mercy of "the quack, the charlatan, the jingo **and** the terrorist."

With media, as with almost every single one of our problems, we need better, smarter organizing at every level and a willingness on the part of liberals and leftists to work with what remains of the center to initiate reforms that are a beginning, rather than an end, in the process of societal transformation. As American history consistently instructs us, this is pretty much the only way things change in our system. New Deal, and to a less extent Great Society, legislation notwithstanding, progressive reform has always proved extraordinarily difficult in America and has almost always arrived piecemeal. Moreover, because our system makes it so much easier to obstruct than to construct, conservatives almost always appear to be in the driver's seat. Barack Obama was right, once again, when he reminded supporters in 2010,

"It took time to free the slaves. It took time for women to get the vote. It took time for workers to get the right to organize." Over time, these reforms added up to a kind of revolution that succeeded without bloodshed or widespread destruction of order, property, or necessary institutions. The key words for liberals and progressives to remember, however, are "over time."

Finally, one hypothesis for the Obama administration's willingness to compromise so extensively on the promises that candidate Obama made during the 2008 campaign—one I'm tempted to share, I'll admit, only on my most optimistic days—is that as president he is playing for time. Obama is taking the best deal on the table today but hopes and expects that once he is reelected in 2012, he will build on the foundations laid during his first term to bring on the fundamental "change" not possible in today's environment. This would be consistent with FDR's strategy during his second term and makes a kind of sense when one considers the nature of the opposition Obama faces today and the likelihood that it will discredit itself before the 2012 election. For that strategy to make sense, however, 2013 will have to provide a more pregnant sense of progressive possibility than 2009 did, and that will take a great deal of work by the rest of us. In other words, the election of 2008 was hardly the culmination of our efforts to "change" America, merely their beginning. For that to become a reality, the president will have to change the way he both imagines and executes his responsibilities as president; so too, the rest of us, as citizens of the world's oldest continuing (and continually self-renewing) democratic republic. To borrow from Hillel the Elder: "If not now, when? If not us, who?"

EPILOGUE

The Thrill Is Gone

The political consequences of the events described in this work proved dire for the Obama administration. No president could hope to see his party succeed in a midterm election where unemployment hovered near 10 percent—and was actually over 16 percent if the people who had given up entirely on finding a job were counted. But the scope of the shellacking that took place on November 2, 2010, far exceeded what might have been expected based on purely exogenous factors. The influential election model created by venerable economist Douglas Hibbs Jr., for instance, based on a number of factors that focus on measures of perceived per capita income growth and disposable income among voters, predicted a 45-seat loss in the House of Representatives. But the Democrats lost at least 60 seats and would likely have lost the Senate had Republican primary voters not chosen so many obviously unqualified candidates holding so many bizarre political views. At the crucial local level, where state and federal redistricting maps will be drawn and will therefore shape future national elections for the coming decade, Republicans picked up 680 state legislative seats, smashing the previous record of 628 by the Democrats in the post-Watergate election of 1974, and the Republicans' best showing since 1928. This was the Democrats' worst performance, in the party's history. How to explain it?

"Historians will puzzle over the fact that Barack Obama, the best communicator of his generation, totally lost control of the narrative in his first year in office and allowed people to view something they had voted for as something they suddenly didn't want," predicted political scientist James Morone. "Communication was the one thing everyone thought Obama would be able to master." And certainly, as Barack Obama observed to *Rolling Stone*, "In an ideal world, I wouldn't have inherited a $1.3 trillion deficit and the worst recession since the Great Depression. But you work with what's before you." Indeed, on Inauguration Day 2009 the unemployment rate was raging out of control as the economy hemorrhaged, on average, 800,000 jobs per month. According to the nonpartisan Congressional Budget Office, the president's emergency stimulus bill helped to create or preserve 3.7 million jobs. The tax cuts contained in the bill saved nearly $1,200 for 97 percent of U.S. households. Moreover, Obama's health care reform bill, his financial reform bill, and the saving of the auto industry made his first two years as president among the most politically consequential in the past half-century—far exceeding the accomplishments of his immediate Democratic predecessors, Bill Clinton and Jimmy Carter.

But Barack Obama expected these achievements to somehow speak for themselves. In doing so, he forgot, as Henry Louis Mencken liked to say, that nobody ever went broke overestimating the ignorance of the American people (or their impatience). According to a poll published in *Politico* just before the midterm elections, only 23 percent of those polled thought Congress had accomplished more than usual, and a *New York Times*/CBS News found fewer than 10 percent of Americans knew they'd gotten a tax cut, not even a third the number who were under the misimpression that their tax bite had gone up. And how is it, one might fairly ask, that a 47–42 plurality told Bloomberg pollsters that they favored the repeal of the Obama health care reform bill, but three-quarters of the very same people polled supported a ban on insurance companies denying coverage due to pre-existing conditions, 67 percent supported allowing children up to age twenty-six to stay on their parents' policies, and 73 percent wanted to keep more prescription-drug benefits for those on Medicare? A laid-off steelworker from Martins Ferry, Ohio, sadly, spoke for many when he told a *New York Times* reporter, "We heard everything was going to change, but there hasn't been much change and the unemployment is still bad and the area we live in is still really depressed."

Unfortunately, ignorance and impatience often combine in the American public—and the American press—with aggressive ahistoricism, a problem that particularly afflicts progressives. Barack Obama is often unfavorably compared to Franklin Roosevelt by many on the left who forget that Roosevelt was pushed from the left by a genuine mass movement, whereas Barack Obama is facing the opposite. What's more, Obama enjoyed nothing like the kinds of majorities that jump-started the New Deal. In the House, Roosevelt had 322 Democrats and 10 Progressives and Farmer-Laborites against 103 Republicans, whereas Obama's supermajority was the bare minimum of 60 at best, 59 at crucial moments, and it included any number of Blue Dog Democrats. Franklin Roosevelt had 69 in 1934.

Within the Obama administration, explanations tend to take on a self-congratulatory hue. As the president himself told the *New York Times*'s Peter Baker, "There is probably a perverse pride in my administration—and I take responsibility for this; this was blowing from the top—that we were going to do the right thing, even if short-term it was unpopular." One can see the political cost of this attitude regarding the stimulus tax cuts. Not only were these a Republican-friendly way of goosing the economy; also the cuts were actually hidden to most voters because they took the form merely of reducing the tax bite out of earners' regular paychecks, on the theory that this would be the quickest and most efficient way to put money in people's pockets. Too bad most people—as the just-cited polls indicated—never noticed. Ditto Obama's willingness to withhold many of the benefits of the health care reform bill until 2014 in order to keep costs down while inviting insurance companies to take advantage of some of its most profitable provisions right away. Principled? Perhaps. Politically foolish? Undoubtedly.

These and other unforced political errors were compounded by the nature of the team that Obama picked to deal with the crisis. Chief of Staff Rahm Emanuel was deeply invested not only in business-as-usual dealmaking in Congress, as if some other presidential candidate in the race had run on a platform of the single word "Change." The centrist advisers that Obama chose to tackle the financial crisis included Clinton's former Treasury secretary Lawrence Summers, former head of the New York Federal Reserve Bank Timothy Geithner, and the Bush-appointed head of the Federal Reserve Band, Ben Bernanke, whose loyalties lay more with Wall Street bankers than with the Obama administration, much less the millions of unemployed and soon-to-be-unemployed Americans, many of whom were facing foreclosure on their homes. Indeed, for all the inclusiveness of the Obama presidential campaign, he has run one of the tightest, most insulated political operations in modern White House history.

Barack Obama's inability to express much of the phony emotions on cue that Americans—and particularly the members of the American media—have come to expect from their leaders may have compounded his political predicament in this regard. But had the president sent a different signal down "from the top," it is hardly likely that it would have mattered to this core group of advisers, so eager were they to placate Wall Street, Blue Dog Democrats, and the financial players who had caused this horrific mess in the first place. Bankers, not taxpayers, were understood to be the primary constituency of this team, based on its belief that economic recovery rested first and foremost on the restoration of credit flows. And although the point itself is arguable, the politics proved catastrophic.

These choices were accompanied by some extremely ill-advised—indeed, near suicidal—complaints about the lack of appreciation

administration figures were receiving from the administration's political base. Liberals were "fucking retarded," complained Emanuel when
some objected to the administration's failure to fight for a "public option" in the health care reform bill. (Emanuel later apologized to retarded people and their families, but not, alas to liberals.) "They will
be satisfied when we have Canadian healthcare and we've eliminated
the Pentagon. That's not reality," complained spokesman Robert Gibbs
regarding the same topic. And Obama himself joshed at a late autumn,
$30,000 per person fund-raiser at the Greenwich, Connecticut, "If we
get an historic health-care bill passed—oh, well, the public option
wasn't there. If you get the financial-reform bill passed—then, well, I
don't know about this particular derivatives rule, I'm not sure that I'm
satisfied with that. And gosh, we haven't yet brought about world
peace and—(laughter) I thought that was going to happen quicker."

Perhaps Obama and company were reflecting the casual disdain
that so many in the Washington establishment feel toward dedicated
campaign supporters, both in local communities and the blogosphere,
but if so, the foolishness they evinced in repeatedly giving voice to
this disdain is breathtaking in its insularity and arrogance. It is
Politics 101, for goodness' sakes, not to insult your own base, particularly as you are about to face an election in which you are already suf-
fering from a massive "enthusiasm gap" vis-à-vis your highly
motivated adversary. And it was not trash talk on the part of Obama
and his advisers. This was the policy as well. The head of a large liberal organization who claimed to have raised millions for the Obama
campaign, according to Edward Luce of the *Financial Times*, complained that he and his colleagues were treated by the White House
"as though we are children. . . . Our advice is never sought. We are
only told: 'This is the message, please get it out.'"

The opening act of the Obama presidency was based on two strategic premises. First, in what might be called the "Rodney King Plan,"
Obama would say to the Republicans, "Why Can't We All Just Get

Along?" and turn down the dial on his side's rhetoric from eleven to two or three. Second, this presidency would Get Things Done: big things, things that no other modern president could manage and, somehow, do them pretty much all at the same time. To do this, he needed to compromise on virtually every one of his campaign promises. The scale and scope of the various emergencies facing the country—particularly given its rapidly rising unemployment and frozen capital flows—did not allow for the luxury of making good on his promise to transform the manner in which business was conducted. Voters, Obama's inner circle widely assumed, would understand.

But Obama badly misjudged the willingness of Republicans to treat actual governance as their responsibility. He wasted months and months in pursuit of bipartisan support that was never going to materialize and in constructing what may have been unnecessary and counterproductive compromise proposals that were adopted largely for their likelihood to appeal to a group of chimerical Republican "moderates," almost all of whom felt far too threatened by the rise of the "Tea Party" extremists in their districts even to contemplate cooperation with America's foreign-born, Commie/Nazi/Muslim/death-panel-imposing phony-baloney president. And so, by sticking to this strategy, the president weakened his legislation, alienated his supporters, and was repaid with little but mockery and contempt from those whose support he continued to seek.

This problem was evident from the beginning. Three days after the 2008 presidential election, in a column entitled "Franklin Delano Obama?" Nobel laureate economist Paul Krugman advised the Obama administration "to figure out how much help they think the economy needs, then add 50 percent. It's much better, in a depressed economy, to err on the side of too much stimulus than on the side of too little."

Yet Obama did just the opposite. His own chair of the Council of Economic Advisers, Christina Romer, calculated that at least $1.2 trillion worth of stimulus spending would be necessary to produce a genuine recovery, and this was a conservative estimate. But Obama fought to keep the figure under $900 billion and insisted that much of this be given over to tax cuts. Krugman, among many other economists, including his fellow Nobel laureate Joseph Stiglitz, judged the Obama stimulus package to be insufficient to the task at hand. Obama did not dispute the substance of this complaint, only its practicality. As his chief of staff, Rahm Emanuel, told the *New Yorker*'s Ryan Lizza, these economists had "never worked the legislative process. . . . My view is that Krugman as an economist is not wrong. But in the art of the possible, of the deal, he is wrong. He couldn't get his legislation."

In fact, history has borne out the Krugman/Stiglitz complaint. Not only was the stimulus too small to inspire the kind of economic rebound that might have given Democrats a fighting chance in this election, but also the willingness of the White House to make the stimulus Republican-friendly ensured that people would barely notice what positive effects it may have had. The enormous emphasis on tax cuts—like the ones 90 percent of Americans have never heard of—rather than, say, on a green jobs program like mass transit investment or school construction—represented not only a failure of policy but one of politics as well, as it sacrificed a golden opportunity to help voters define Obama and the Democrats in ways that distinguished them from their political adversaries in a positive, meaningful fashion. But repeatedly during his first two years, Obama watered down his goals without winning any Republican cooperation in the process. In doing so, he alienated his own side, and he failed to protect virtually any of the Blue Dogs Emanuel had worked so hard to recruit—the vast majority of whom lost their seats on November 2, 2010.

All this was consistent with Obama's belief in taking the "ham sandwich" when the "whole hog" proved unavailable. And in another time, it might have worked. But thanks to Fox News, talk radio, and the incipient Tea Party takeover of the Republican Party, among other unhappy manifestations of what Philip Roth has aptly termed "the indigenous American berserk," American politics had traveled too far down the road toward "invincible ignorance" to allow anyone, much less an African-American president with a name like "Barack Hussein Obama," to traffic in the reasoned language of compromise and cooperation understandably favored by the onetime president of the *Harvard Law Review*, now president of the United States. And the Republicans could hardly have been less interested. Just in case anyone had any illusions on this point, Mitch McConnell, the Senate minority leader, helpfully explained, "The single most important thing we want to achieve is for President Obama to be a one-term president."

Yet Obama never admitted any of the above. Faced with a media establishment that treats Fox News as, well, "news" and considers Newt Gingrich as a sage, Obama bought into the blithe Beltway pretense that Republicans were acting in good faith and that it was those pesky liberals who needed to be kept in line. And by taking whatever deal was available to him and mocking those on the left (and in the center) who took his campaign promises seriously, Obama not only alienated specific constituencies whose electoral support had been conditional on progress being made in areas of special concern; he also implicitly repudiated the very spirit of his historic candidacy—the spirit that had inspired people to commit themselves to his cause.

As longtime educator and organizer Marshall Ganz observed in the aftermath of the November 2010 debacle, "President Obama entered office wrapped in a mantle of moral leadership. His call for change was rooted in values that had long been eclipsed in our public life: a sense of mutual responsibility, commitment to equality and belief in inclusive diversity. Those values inspired a new generation of voters, restored faith to the cynical and created a national movement. Now, 18 months and an 'enthusiasm gap' later, the nation's major challenges remain largely unmet, and a discredited conservative movement has reinvented itself in a more virulent form."

Borrowing categorical distinctions originally mapped out by political scientist James MacGregor Burns in the late 1970s, Ganz (who had played a role in mapping out the original organizing strategy for the Obama campaign) assessed that immediately upon becoming president, Obama had abandoned the "transformational" political model promised by his presidential campaign in favor of a "transactional" model. "'Transformational leadership,'" Ganz explained "engages followers in the risky and often exhilarating work of changing the world, work that often changes the activists themselves. Its sources are shared values that become wellsprings of the courage, creativity and hope needed to open new pathways to success. 'Transactional' leadership, on the other hand, is about horse-trading, operating within the routine, and it is practiced to maintain, rather than change, the status quo."

The nation was ready for the former, Ganz insisted, but Obama picked the latter. And so "much of the public's anger, disappointment and frustration has been turned on a leader who failed to lead." Ganz identified "three crucial choices that undermined the president's transformational mission": "First, he abandoned the bully pulpit of moral argument and public education. Next, he chose to lead with a politics of compromise rather than advocacy. And finally, he chose to demobilize the movement that elected him president. By shifting focus from a public ready to drive change—as in 'yes we can'—he shifted the focus to himself and attempted to negotiate change from the inside, as in 'yes I can.'"

As a result of these choices, Obama not only failed to convince the public that he could turn around the economy—the central political axis upon which judgment of the success or failure of his presidency turned—but he also lost the confidence of many of his original supporters. True, the president operated from the disadvantage of a particularly "cool" communications style. (Though one cannot help but wonder how these same White House reporters would have treated the sight of an angry black man screaming and pounding the lectern before the cameras.) But in his refusal to adapt the inspirational rhetoric of his campaign to his presidency, he allowed the forces of right-wing reaction to claim the mantle of the common man. They even managed to make it appear to most people as if the Democrats, rather than the Republicans, were the party in the pocket of Wall Street and the big-spending fat cats. And as to the "success" of Obama's policies in averting a far greater catastrophe, these are, as political scientist Thomas Mann observes, "invisible to a public reacting to the here and now, not to the counterfactual of how much worse it might have been."

It's hard to know whether Obama's legislative record could have been improved by a more savvy political strategy that dispensed with the misguided reliance on Republican reasonableness suddenly manifesting itself somewhere down the road. What is easy to imagine is a much stronger showing for Democrats in the 2010 election and beyond, and with it, the possibility of building on the achievements of the previous two years. The 2010 exit polls tell many stories for progressives, none of them particularly heartening. The number of self-described "conservative" voters increased from 32 percent in 2006 to 41 percent in 2010, the largest percentage in twenty years. Independents switched their allegiance from a 57–39 Democratic margin to a 55–39 Republican one four years later as well. But a key component of this unhappy tale can be found in the votes of those who remained in the Democratic camp, specifically young people and minorities. As Ruy Teixeira and John Halpin of the Center for American Progress Action Fund observe, the "youth vote" was one of the few categories of voters to stick with Democrats in 2010. "Young people aged 18–29 years old supported Democrats by a 13-point margin in the 2010 election (55 percent to 42 percent)." This was not as lopsided as the 63–34 margin Democrats got from young people in 2008, nor did it equal the 60–38 percent level of 2006. But the big difference between those elections and 2008 was turnout. Roughly 11 percent of 2010 voters were eighteen to twenty-nine years of age, well below their 18 percent share in 2008 and even below their pre-Obama levels of participation in 2006. Meanwhile, minority voters declined as a percentage of voters by 4 percentage points from their 2008 level, a rare and unusual occurrence, particularly given the fact that the success or failure of America's first minority president rested on its results.

Part of the explanation for the evident disillusion must lie with unrealistic expectation for first-time voters. But the disappearance of the heroic narrative of the campaign and its replacement with an ongoing series of back-room dealings of exactly the kind of candidate Obama so eloquently condemned must be apportioned a lion's share of the blame. Imagine if young people and first-time voters heard their president sounding like the candidate who told his audience, upon securing the Democratic nomination for president, "We will be able to look back and tell our children that this was the moment when we began to provide care for the sick and good jobs to the jobless; this was the moment when the rise of the oceans began to slow and our planet began to heal; this was the moment when we ended a war and secured our nation and restored our image as the last, best hope on earth."

Early in 2005, the newly seated junior senator from Illinois—Barack Obama—invited me to come to Washington to join him for dinner with a small group of the heads of Washington's most influential progressive organizations. It was a pretty depressed group, given the outcome of the election that had just taken place. This exciting, young, African-American's inspiring keynote speech at the convention that August, coupled with his subsequent landslide senate victory, were pretty much the only good news anybody had seen in the previous year's politics.

The contents of what was said during that meeting must remain confidential, but I don't think I'd be violating any rules if I admitted that, after being seated next to Obama for the course of the evening, I came away deeply impressed by his poise, his self-confidence, and his intelligence. In profound contrast to virtually every Democratic politician with national ambitions at the time, Obama did not evince even the slightest concern about his ability to connect with culturally conservative and deeply religious Americans. But he was worried about his own—and his party's—inability to offer a coherent response to the economic transformation underway in America. Long before the Wall Street crash, when housing prices were still high and most middle-class Americans felt themselves to be on relatively secure ground, Obama was looking for a way to address the problems of scores of workers being undercut and eventually displaced by global competition. He knew how to talk to people in church; it was outside the locked factory gates in towns where the jobs had moved overseas where he felt himself stymied. And as he sat down to write the draft of what would become his second book, *The Audacity of Hope*, he thought some of the people in the room might have some ideas worth exploring.

I don't remember if anyone had anything useful to offer that night. If they did, it wasn't much. I do know that if you ask most Americans what conservatives believe will address America's economic ills, they can give you a simple, coherent response: lower taxes, less government, more "freedom." It may be wrong. It may benefit only the wealthiest among us. And it is not only easy to understand; it has been repeated in lockstep now for nearly half a century, with literally billions of dollars spent to make it appear plausible. It's not merely that conservatives are better than conservatives at selling their product, or that they happen to have an easier—and undoubtedly simpler—ideological product to sell. It's that they know what they are selling. Much of what Tea Party candidates claimed about the world and the global economy during the 2010 election would have earned their adherents a well-deserved "F" in any half-decent freshman economics or earth science class. But it was a story that enough voters could connect to their circumstances and their fears to allow themselves to trust these charlatans with the future of their government. Liberals do not suffer from the sin of "invincible ignorance" when it comes to addressing America's problems, and so do not appear to address potential solutions with anything like the far right's aura of God-given self-confidence. They understand that our problems are complex and spring from myriad causes, and that the responses to them must be appropriate in approach and scale. That is undoubtedly a disadvantage with some voters, but it is one that can be at least partially offset by presenting a plausible story about how our policies and plans can be expected to provide America's citizens (and their children) with a brighter future than the one they feel they face today. To achieve this, however, will require considerable re-imagination regarding our story about how the world works and what, exactly, is America's place in its future. We cannot depend on having presidents as obviously clueless and incompetent as the first George Bush, or as arrogant, incompetent, and ideologically driven as the second one to lay the groundwork for all Democratic victories in the future. These catastrophes may return, of course. (And given the current crop of potential Republican presidential candidates, beginning with Sarah Palin, they presently appear more likely than not.) But elections won purely on the basis of America's rejections of the other guy do not begin to provide the necessary foundation upon which to build a long-term progressive future. Slogans like "Hope" and "Change" can help win elections, but they are not much in governing; for that, a president and a party must have a vision, or they shall surely perish.

All presidents make errors that appear obvious in retrospect. Barack Obama had better information than the rest of us do about the issues he faced and sensible reasons for most of the choices he made. He is, after all, the same fellow who ran the brilliant and inspirational 2008 campaign for the presidency that looked as if it could transform both the form and content of American politics. But if the previous pages prove anything at all, it is that change is a great deal more difficult to achieve than it appears on the surface. The system itself stands in its way. And although "hope" is a necessary condition for "change," it nowhere near enough given the strength of the forces arrayed on behalf of America's corrupt and sclerotic status quo.

But Obama's mistakes in office are nowhere near the entire story of the rise and fall of progressive hopes during the first two years of his presidency. We must all shoulder our share of the blame as well. A few days after the 2010 midterm election, Van Jones, the African-American environmental activist who served briefly in the Obama administration before being forced out over some silly statements he had made years earlier, spoke to a progressive gathering in Washington, DC. After recalling the pageant of progressive performers who came to Washington to celebrate Obama's Inaugural inauguration at the Lincoln Memorial which featured, among many others, Bono, Bruce Springsteen, Beyoncé, Stevie Wonder, Pete Seeger and the Gay Men's Chorus of Washington, Jones reminded his listeners, "You had the full beauty of the American people, the full force of our culture on display. . . . None of those people quit the movement and joined the Tea Party. All that creativity, all that power, all that spirit, all that soul—it's still here. We went from We Are One to We Are Done. Well, guess what? The days are now over when any of us can afford to wait for a politician in Washington, DC, to set the tone and the tenor and the face of our movement."

The essential ingredient missing from Obama's campaign of hope and change was the hard work that would be necessary from all of us to convert the former into the latter; not only on his part, but on ours as well.

NOTES

INTRODUCTION

1   **govern in prose**: Kevin Sack, "Cuomo the Orator Now Soliloquizes in Book Form; Disclaiming Greatness, He Labors On: An Embryonic Idea Here, an Honorarium There," *New York Times*, September 27, 1993, www.nytimes.com/1993/09/27/nyregion/cuomo-orator-now-soliloquizes-book-form-disclaiming-greatness-he-labors.html; Mario Cuomo, *More Than Words: The Speeches of Mario Cuomo* (New York: St Martin's Press, 1993).

1   **preserving women's rights**: Barack Obama, *Change We Can Believe In: Barack Obama's Plan to Renew America's Promise* (New York: Crown, 2008), 167.

2   **an insurance exchange**: Barack Obama, "Weekly Address: President Obama Says Health Care Reform Cannot Wait," White House, July 18, 2009, www.whitehouse.gov/the_press_office/Weekly-Address-President-Obama-Says-Health-Care-Reform-Cannot-Wait/.

2   **Employee Free Choice Act**: Barack Obama, "The Obama-Biden Plan," Obama's campaign Web site, http://change.gov/agenda/economy_agenda/.

2   **all carbon emissions**: Barack Obama, "Remarks of Senator Barack Obama: Real Leadership for a Clean Energy Future," Organizing for America, October 8, 2010, www.barackobama.com/2007/10/08/remarks_of_senator_barack_obam_28.php.

2   **common-sense regulations**: Barack Obama, "Remarks of Senator Barack Obama," Organizing for America, October 18, 2010, http://my.barackobama.com/page/community/post/stateupdates/gGg2xq.

2   **promises made by John McCain**: Jimmy Fallon, "Laugh Lines," *New York Times*, November 15, 2009, http://query.nytimes.com/gst/fullpage.html?res=9B04EFD6143EF936A25752C1A96F9C8B63.

2   **overplayed their hand**: Gerald F. Seib, "Voters' Faith Deficit Widens," *Wall Street Journal*, May 25, 2010, http://online.wsj.com/article/SB10001424052748704792104575264401008018866.html.

3   **repudiate the left**: Clive Crook, "Obama Has Angered the Centre and the Left," *Financial Times*, July 18, 2010, www.ft.com/cms/s/0/95af8f36-9295-11df-9142-00144feab49a.html.

3   **most radical president:** Adam J. Rose, "Gingrich: Obama 'Most Radical President in American History,'" Huffington Post, April 9, 2010, www.huffingtonpost.com/2010/04/09/gingrich-obama-most-radic_n_531343.html; Robert Costa, "Gingrich: Obama's 'Kenyan, Anti-Colonial' Worldview," *National Review Online*, September 11, 2010, www.nationalreview.com/corner/246302/gingrich-obama-s-kenyan-anti-colonial-worldview-robert-costa.

3   **grab for half the loaf**: Ross Douthat, "The Obama Way," *New York Times*, December 25, 2009, www.nytimes.com/2009/12/26/opinion/26douthat.html.

3   **the trajectory of American politics**: "Obama: Reagan Changed Direction; Bill Clinton Didn't," YouTube, January 21, 2008, www.youtube.com/watch?v=HFLuOBsNMZA.

3   **the whole hog**: David Remnick, *The Bridge: The Life and Rise of Barack Obama* (New York: Random House, 2010), 304.

4   **a nation healed:** Edward Luce, "Obama's Fearsome Foursome," *Financial Times*, February 6, 2010, www.businessspectator.com.au/bs.nsf/Article/Obamas-fearsome-foursome-pd20100205-2D3U7?OpenDocument&src=sph.

CHAPTER ONE

7   **age of forgetting**: Tony Judt, *Reappraisals: Reflections on the Forgotten Twentieth Century* (New York: Penguin, 2008), 1.

7   **an extraordinary burden of problems**: Joseph Stiglitz and Linda Bilmes, "The Three Trillion Dollar War," *Times Online*, February 23, 2008, www.timesonline.co.uk/tol/comment/columnists/guest_contributors/article3419840.ece.

8   **theory of the unitary executive**: "The President's Moment," *New York Times*, June 12, 2010, www.nytimes.com/2010/06/13/opinion/13sun1.html.

8   **Bush's dereliction:** Thomas B. Edsall, "The Rove Legacy," *Democracy*, Summer 2010, www.democracyjournal.org/ article.php?ID=6754.

9   **lowest level of job creation:** Ibid.

9   **with 535 members:** Barack Obama, "Couric Exclusive Interview with President Obama," Katie Couric, *CBS News*, February 7, 2010, www.cbsnews.com/video/watch/?id=6184114n.

9   **play the cards:** Jann S. Wenner, "Obama in Command: The Rolling Stone Interview," *Rolling Stone online*, September 28, 2010, www.rollingstone.com/politics/news/17390/209395?RS_show_page =0, 4.

10   **much of our physical infrastructure:** "Poor Infrastructure Fails America, Civil Engineers Report," CNN, January 29, 2009, articles.cnn.com/2009-01-28/us/infrastructure.report.card_1_ drinking-water-infrastructure-aging?_s=PM:US.

10   **streetlights in some places:** Michael Cooper, "Governments Go to Extremes as the Downturn Wears On," *New York Times*, August 6, 2010, www.nytimes.com/2010/08/07/us/07cutbacksWEB.html ?pagewanted=1&_r=1.

10   **inland waterways, wastewater systems, levees:** Andrew Restuccia, "Oil and Gas Industry Writes Its Own Pipeline Standards," *Washington Independent*, August 13, 2010, http://washington independent.com/94743/oil-and-gas-industry-writes-its-own- pipeline-standards.

10   **an appalling apathy:** Jodi Enda, "Capital Flight," *American Journalism Review Online*, June/July 2010, www.ajr.org/Article.asp ?id=4877.

11   **responsible for his administration's reaction:** Ryan Lizza, "As the World Burns," *New Yorker*, October 11, 2010, www.newyorker .com/reporting/2010/10/11/101011fa_fact_lizza.

11   **the president's position:** Peggy Noonan, "He Was Supposed to Be Competent," *Wall Street Journal*, May 29, 2010, online.wsj.com/ article/SB10001424052748704269204575270950789108846.html

11   **take a look:** Enda, "Capital Flight."

12   **no enforcement mechanisms:** David Barstow, Laura Dodd, James Glamz, Stephanie Saul, and Ian Urbina, "Regulators Failed to

Address Risks in Oil Rig Fail-Safe Device," *New York Times*, June 20, 2010, www.nytimes.com/2010/06/21/us/21blowout .html?src=twt&twt=nytimes.

12   **generally accepted practice:** Ian Urbina, "Inspector General's Inquiry Faults Regulators," *New York Times*, May 24, 2010, www.nytimes.com/2010/05/25/us/25mms.html.

12   **200 violations of its regulations:** Alex Seitz-Wald, "Despite Finding 200 Violations in Gulf Drilling Operations over the Past Five Years, MMS Collected Only 16 Fines," ThinkProgress, June 9, 2010, http://thinkprogress.org/2010/06/09/mms -on-the-job/.

12   **paid little attention:** Abrahm Lustgarten and Ryan Knutson (ProPublica), "Reports at BP Over Years Find History of Problems," *Washington Post*, June 8, 2010, www.washingtonpost.com/wp-dyn/content/article/2010/06/07/AR2010060704826.html.

12   **less than reliable deepwater well design:** Russell Gold and Tom McGinty, "BP Relied on Cheaper Wells," *Wall Street Journal*, June 19, 2010, http://online.wsj.com/article/SB100014240527487 04289504575313010283981200.html.

12   **the blowout preventer rams:** Ian Urbina, "Workers on Doomed Rig Voiced Concern About Safety," *New York Times*, July 21, 2010, www.nytimes.com/2010/07/22/us/22transocean.html.

13   **390 overdue maintenance problems:** Sheila McNulty, "BP Listed 390 problems on Gulf Rig," *Financial Times*, August 23, 2010, www.ft.com/cms/s/0/7d66d5aa-aee3-11df-8e45-00144feabdc0.html.

13   **Transocean was still refusing:** Harry R. Weber, "Panel: Transocean Not Providing Oil Spill Documents," Salon, October 5, 2010, www.salon.com/news/feature/2010/10/05/us_gulf_oil_spill_ investigation_2.

13   **released huge amounts of toxic chemicals:** Ibid.

14   **BP did not alert local officials:** James McKinley Jr., "With Neighbors Unaware, Toxic Spill at a BP Plant," *New York Times*, August 29, 2010, www.nytimes.com/2010/08/30/us/ 30bprefinery.html.

14   **Bush/Cheney deputy secretary**: Paul Krugman, "Sex &
      Drugs & the Spill," *New York Times*, May 9, 2010,
      www.nytimes.com/2010/05/10/opinion/10krugman.html.

15   **Dick Cheney Energy Bill**: Joshua Dorner, "The Prelude to
      Cheney's Katrina," Center for American Progress, June 4, 2010,
      www.americanprogress.org/issues/2010/06/prelude_cheney_katrina
      .html.

16   **this ideology's ruinous effects**: Ibid.

CHAPTER TWO

17   **the self-critical element:** Jann S. Wenner, "Obama in Command:
      The Rolling Stone Interview," *Rolling Stone,* September 28, 2010,
      www.rollingstone.com/politics/news/17390/209395.

17   **unemployment figure reached 9.5 percent:** Daniel J. Weiss,
      "Anatomy of a Senate Climate Bill Death," Center for American
      Progress, October 12, 2010, www.americanprogress.org/issues/
      2010/10/senate_climate_bill.html; ": Mokoto Rich, "U.S. Lost
      131,000 Jobs as Government Cuts Back," *New York Times*, August
      6, 2010.

18   **at the federal Congressional level:** David Roberts, "The Real
      Reason the Climate Change Bill Is Going to Suck," grist.org,
      November 2, 2009, www.grist.org/article/2009-11-02-the-real-
      reason-the-climate-bill-is-going-to-suck.

19   **sitting pretty faction:** Ron Elving, "Beneath NPR's Poll, the
      'Tyranny of Constituency,'" NPR, June 18, 2010, www.npr.org/
      blogs/watchingwashington/2010/06/18/127926122/watching
      washington.

19   **exercise far more party discipline:** Roberts, "The Real Reason."

19   **knife fights carrying library books:** Jennifer Medina, "Style
      Differences on Display as 4 Mayoral Rivals Debate," *New York
      Times*, May 16, 2005, http://query.nytimes.com/gst/fullpage.html
      ?res=9E00E0DF1F30F935A25756C0A9639C8B63&sec=&spon=
      &pagewanted=all.

19   **Abercrombie was already gone:** Michael Tomasky, "Just Shoot
      Me," *The Guardian*, March 5, 2010,

www.guardian.co.uk/commentisfree/michaeltomasky/2010/mar/05/congress-democrats.

20   **the United States and South Africa:** John Micklethwait and Adrian Wooldridge, *The Right Nation: Conservative Power in America* (New York: Penguin Press, 2004), 7.

20   **no checkups or vaccinations:** Nicholas Kristof, "The Larger Shame," *New York Times,* September 6, 2005.

20   **infant-mortality rates:** Malcolm Gladwell, "The Moral-Hazard Myth," *New Yorker,* August 29, 2005, www.newyorker.com/archive/2005/08/29/050829fa_fact.

20   **the party of Hell, no!:** Jeff Zeleny, "Republicans Weighing Party's Message," *New York Times,* April 9, 2010, www.nytimes.com/2010/04/10/us/politics/10memo.html.

21   **DeMint found it necessary:** Eric Alterman, "Think Again: Forget the Question. The Answer Is 'Tax Cuts,'" Center for American Progress, September 9, 2010, www.americanprogress.org/issues/2010/09/ta090910.html.

21   **the nonpartisan Congressional Budget Office:** David Kocieniewski, "Tax Cuts May Prove Better for Politicians Than for Economy," *New York Times,* September 10, 2010, www.nytimes.com/2010/09/11/business/economy/11tax.html.

21   **I don't need to see GDP numbers:** "John Boehner's Anti-intellectualism," YouTube, August 1, 2010, www.youtube.com/watch?v=yeD-1iRQDDM.

21   **they increased revenue:** Steve Benen, "When an Entire Political Party Moves to Bizarroland," *Washington Monthly,* July 14, 2010, www.washingtonmonthly.com/archives/individual/2010_07/024712.php.

22   **Ed Lazear:** Ezra Klein, "The Failure of Conservative Elites," *Washington Post,* July 14, 2010, http://voices.washingtonpost.com/ezra-klein/2010/07/the_failure_of_conservative_el.html.

22   **two most consequential policies:** Ezra Klein, "The GOP's Bad Idea," *Washington Post,* September 23, 2010, http://voices.washingtonpost.com/ezra-klein/2010/09/the_gops_bad_idea.html.

22   **ditto the call for reductions:** Ibid.

23   **a naive moral relativism:** Jacob Heilbrunn, "End of the
      Establishment," *Foreign Policy*, July–August 2010, www.foreign
      policy.com/articles/2010/07/16/end_of_the_establishment?hide
      comments=yes.

23   **Pledge to America:** "'Pledge to America' Unveiled by Republicans
      (Full Text)", CBSnews.com, September 22, 2010,
      www.cbsnews.com/8301-503544_162-20017335-503544.html.

24   **barely a third disagreed:** Shannon Travis, "CNN Poll: Quarter
      Doubt Obama Was Born in U.S.," CNN.com, August 4, 2010,
      http://politicalticker.blogs.cnn.com/2010/08/04/cnn-poll-quarter-
      doubt-president-was-born-in-u-s/?fbid=zUY96GSzIn6#_
      rndmva11234=&more-116389.

24   **a week into his presidency:** Norman Ornstein, "Ending the
      Permanent Campaign," *The Nation*, August 12, 2010,
      www.thenation.com/article/154016/ending-permanent-campaign.

24   **Senator DeMint famously promised:** "Sen. Jim DeMint Calls
      Defeating Obama Like Waterloo," YouTube, July 20, 2009,
      www.youtube.com/watch?v=mHV4nDS501Y.

24   **entirely irrelevant to anyone's calculations:** Norman Ornstein,
      "Obama: A Pragmatic Moderate Faces the 'Socialist' Smear,"
      Washington Post, April 14, 2010, www.washingtonpost.com/
      wp-dyn/content/article/2010/04/13/AR2010041303686.html.

25   **Treasury bonds:** Rhonda B. Graham, "Well-Managed Bailout
      Creates Returns to Help Reduce the Deficit," *News Journal*,
      October 21, 2010, www.delawareonline.com/article/20101021/
      OPINION12/10210334/1004/OPINION.

25   **the ink was dry:** "Arlen Specter Speaks on Health Care," December
      17, 2009, http://specter.senate.gov/public/index.cfm?Fuse
      Action=NewsRoom.ArlenSpecterSpeaks&ContentRecord_id=
      b378a81a-cbad-9915-bc70-661d5ad9b1af&Region_id=&Issue_id=.

25   **a little purer in your ideology:** Lydia DePillis, "Meet the New
      GOP Centrists," *New Republic*, January 13, 2010,
      www.tnr.com/article/politics/meet-the-new-gop-centrists.

25   **every victory gained:** Sun Tzu, *The Art of War*, www.christopher
      morin.org/World%20History/Ancient%20China/ArtofWar.doc.

CHAPTER THREE

27 **when the U.S. Senate was created:** 1790 U.S. Census, 8, www2.census.gov/prod2/decennial/documents/1790m-02.pdf.

27 **that number is seventy times:** U.S. Census Bureau, 2009 U.S. Population Estimates, www.census.gov/popest/states/NST-ann-est.html.

27 **forty Republican senators elected:** Elisabeth Bumiller, "Top Defense Officials Seek to End 'Don't Ask, Don't Tell,'" *New York Times*, February 2, 2010.

28 **African American, Hispanic, or Native American:** Steven Hill, "Washington's House of Lords," E!Sharp, November 29, 2009, www.esharp.eu/Web-specials/Washington-s-House-of-Lords.

28 **average senator spends about 1 percent:** Ezra Klein, "Did the Invention of the Airplane End the Filibuster?" *Washington Post*, November 13, 2009, http://voices.washingtonpost.com/ezra-klein/2009/11/did_the_invention_of_the_airpl.html.

29 **a close corollary:** U.S. Senate Cloture Motions, table, U.S. Senate Reference, www.senate.gov/pagelayout/reference/cloture_motions/clotureCounts.htm.

29 **political scientist Barbara Sinclair:** Ezra Klein, "The Rise of the Filibuster: An Interview with Barbara Sinclair," *Washington Post*, December 26, 2009, http://voices.washingtonpost.com/ezra-klein/2009/12/the_right_of_the_filibuster_an.html.

29 **the Democratic takeover:** U.S. Senate Cloture Motions, table.

30 **fewer than half of Obama's nominees:** Mark Sherman, "Obama Has Fewer Judge Confirmations Than Nixon," Salon, September 6, 2010, www.salon.com/news/feature/2010/09/06/us_obama_judges.

30 **Senator Claire McCaskill:** Zaid Jilani, "Republicans Block Votes on 97 Federal Nominees in a Single Day," ThinkProgress, April 21, 2010, http://thinkprogress.org/2010/04/21/kyl-gop-obstruction-97/.

30 **three CBP commissioners:** James Fallows, "Neustadt Principle in Action: Recess Appointments (Updated)," *Atlantic Monthly*, March 27, 2010, www.theatlantic.com/politics/archive/2010/03/neustadt-principle-in-action-recess-appointments-updated/38120/.

30   **Senator Charles Grassley:** Melanie Trottman and Brody Mullins, "Tensions Flare as Obama Uses Recess Power," (table), *Wall Street Journal*, March 29, 2010, http://online.wsj.com/article/SB1000 14240527023043254045751483332890329718.html.

30   **Richard Shelby:** Kate Phillips and Jeff Zeleny, "White House Blasts Shelby Hold on Nominees," *New York Times*, February 5, 2010, http://thecaucus.blogs.nytimes.com/2010/02/05/white-house-blasts-shelby-hold-on-nominees/.

31   **Royal Swedish Academy of Sciences:** Tom Raum, "Nobel Prize May Not Help Obama's Fed Nominee," Associated Press, October 12, 2010, www.google.com/hostednews/ap/article/ALeqM5iBiaze C6HItyYwqi8BtyzrKo1whwD9IQoK100?docId=D9IQoK100.

31   **Mary Landrieu:** Jonathan Cohn, "Landrieu: I Can Hold Gov't Hostage, Too," *New Republic*, September 29, 2010, www.tnr.com/blog/jonathan-cohn/78036/landrieu-i-can-be-just-irresonsible-the-republicans.

31   **said she was going to retain:** "Landrieu Responds to Obama Administration Decision to Lift Deepwater Drilling Moratorium," Landrieu Press Release, October 12, 2010, http://landrieu.senate.gov/mediacenter/pressreleases/10-12-2010-1.cfm.

31   **Kentucky's Jim Bunning:** David Lightman and Halimah Abdullah, "Who Really Gets Hurt When GOP's Bunning Blocks This Bill?," McClatchy Newspapers, March 1, 2010, www.mcclatchydc.com/2010/03/01/89610/gops-bunning-told-off-senators.html.

32   **Senator Bunning replied:** Jake Sherman and Manu Raju, "Sen. Jim Bunning Holds Floor: 'Tough S—t,'" *Politico*, February 25, 2010, www.politico.com/news/stories/0210/33566.html.

32   **percentage who said the country's problems:** Jon Cohen and Dan Balz, "Beyond the Tea Party," *Washington Post*, October 9, 2010, www.washingtonpost.com/wp-dyn/content/article/2010/10/09/AR2010100903308.html.

32   **slow, quiet, yet inexorable erosion:** Jacob S. Hacker and Paul Pierson, "The Stalemate State," *American Prospect*, October 18, 2010, www.prospect.org/cs/articles?article=the_stalemate_state.

CHAPTER FOUR

33   **nonpartisan Center for Responsive Politics:** "Federal Lobbying Climbs in 2009 as Lawmakers Execute Aggressive Congressional Agenda," Opensecrets.org, http://209.190.229.100/news/2010/02/federal-lobbying-soars-in-2009.html.

33   **lobbies were handing out $20 million:** Ibid.

33   **most generous spreaders of wealth:** Ibid.

33   **PhRMA employed forty-eight lobbying firms:** Paul Blumenthal, "The Legacy of Billy Tauzin: The White House–PhRMA Deal," Sunlight Foundation blog, http://blog.sunlightfoundation.com/2020/02/12/the-legacy-of-billy-tauzin-the-white-house-phrma-deal/.

34   **a quadrillion potential examples:** Sewell Chan, "A Consumer Bill Gives Exemption on Payday Loans," *New York Times*, March 9, 2010, www.nytimes.com/2010/03/10/business/10regulate.html.

34   **a new consumer protection agency:** Ibid.

34   **Citizens for Responsibility and Ethics in Washington:** Ibid.

34   **Jones, his relatives, and his employees:** Ibid.

34   **the industry's campaign contributions to him:** Ibid.

34   **in a denouement:** Sewell Chan, e-mail message to author.

34   **a new consumer bureau:** Ibid.

35   **financial committees in both houses:** Eric Lichtblau and Edward Wyatt, "Financial Overhaul Bill Poses Big Test for Lobbyists," *New York Times*, May 22, 2010, www.nytimes.com/2010/05/23/us/politics/23lobby.html.

35   **fourteen freshmen serving:** "Crew Study: Financial Services Committee a Plum Gig for Freshmen Members of Congress," Center for Responsibility and Ethics in Washington, May 26, 2010, www.citizensforethics.org/node/45080.

35   **Senate Energy and Natural Resources Committee:** John M. Broder and Michael Luo, "Reforms Slow to Arrive at Drilling Agency," *New York Times*, May 30, 2010, www.nytimes.com/2010/05/31/us/politics/31drill.html.

36   **the real outcome of most lobbying:** Melinda Burns, "K Street and the Status Quo," Miller-McCune, August 10, 2010, www.miller-mccune.com/politics/k-street-and-the-status-quo-20015/#.

36   **gridlock and successful stalemating:** Ibid.

37   **a test of foresight:** Jeff Goodell, "As the World Burns," *Rolling Stone*, January 6, 2010, www.rollingstone.com/politics/news/12697/64918?RS_show_page=5.

37   **preemption for the U.S. Chamber of Commerce:** Ryan Lizza, "As the World Burns," *New Yorker*, October 11, 2010, www.newyorker.com/reporting/2010/10/11/101011fa_fact_lizza?currentPage=all.

38   **forces wedded to the old patterns:** Ibid.

38   **the effect of reducing carbon emissions:** Neil deMause, "Sidelining Cap and Trade's Green Critics," FAIR, February 2010, www.fair.org/index.php?page=4005.

38   **even by administration calculations:** Ibid.

39   **top three donors to Peterson's 2008 campaign:** "Representative (D-MN) Collin C. Peterson," Opensecrets.org, www.opensecrets.org/politicians/summary.php?cid=N00004558&cycle=2010

39   **donated $628,687:** Ibid.

39   **lobbyists devoted to climate change:** "The Global Climate Change Lobby," Center for Public Integrity, November 4, 2009, www.publicintegrity.org/investigations/global_climate_change_lobby/key-findings.

39   **138 working on behalf of alternative forms:** Goodell, "As the World Burns."

39   **targets for improving renewable energy resources:** Ibid.

39   **auction off pollution permits:** Ibid.

39   **polluters earned themselves $134 billion:** Ibid.

40   **this awful bill:** Ibid.

40   **global warming is undeniable:** "State of the Climate in 2009," National Oceanic and Atmospheric Administration National Climatic Data Center, www.ncdc.noaa.gov/bams-state-of-the-climate/2009.php.

40   **the influx of greenhouses gases:** "Arctic Ice at All-Time Low," *National Geographic News*, August 20, 2007, http://news.nationalgeographic.com/news/2007/08/070820-global-warming.html.

40   **even the U.S. military:** Bill McKibben, "Hot Mess," *New Republic*, October 6, 2010, www.tnr.com/article/environment-energy/magazine/78208/gop-global-warming-denial-insanity?page=0,2.

40   **the globally averaged temperature:** Ibid.

40   **this new world:** Ibid.
41   **increasing CO2 levels:** Alok Jha, "Copenhagen Climate Summit:
      Five Possible Scenarios for Our Future Climate," *The Guardian,*
      December 18, 2009, www.guardian.co.uk/environment/2009/
      dec/18/copenhagen-five-climate-scenarios.
41   **one-third of the world's species:** Ibid.
41   **global warming may run out of control:** Ibid.
42   **Arctic permafrost enters the danger zone:** Ibid.
42   **offsets and sweeteners and bailouts:** Bill McKibben, "Bringing the
      Heat," *New Republic,* April 5, 2010,
      www.tnr.com/article/politics/bringing-the-heat.
42   **write a check to every American:** Ibid.
42   **gas prices would go up:** James Hansen, "G-8 Failure Reflects U.S.
      Failure on Climate Change," Huffington Post, July 9, 2009,
      www.huffingtonpost.com/dr-james-hansen/g-8-failure-reflects
      -us-f_b_228597.html.
42   **energy-intensive businesses:** McKibben, "Bringing the Heat."
43   **alleged scientific misconduct:** Elizabeth Kolbert, "Up in the Air,"
      New Yorker, April 12, 2010, www.newyorker.com/talk/comment/
      2010/04/12/100412taco_talk_kolbert.
43   **a 2002 memo by the conservative political consultant:** Jane
      Mayer, "Covert Operations," *New Yorker,* August 30, 2010,
      www.newyorker.com/reporting/2020/08/30/100830fa_fact_mayer?
      currentPage=all.
43   **no consensus about global warming:** Ibid.
43   **phase out fossil fuels:** Ibid.
43   **Ed Crane, the institute's founder:** Ibid.
44   **the nearly $200 million:** Ibid.
44   **Koch's personal fortune:** Kate Zernike, "Secretive Republican
      Donors Are Planning Ahead," *New York Times,* October 20, 2010.
44   **Mayer notes:** Mayer, "Covert Operations."
44   **baloney practices:** "Editorial: Hiding Evidence of Global Cooling,"
      Washington Times, November 24, 2009,
      www.washingtontimes.com/news/2009/nov/24/hiding-evidence-of-
      global-cooling.

45   **House of Commons Science and Technology Committee:** Klaus Hasselman, "The Climate Change Game," *Nature Geoscience,* http://www.nature.com/ngeo/journal/v3/n8/full/ngeo919.html.

45   **thanks to climate deniers:** Frank Newport, "Americans' Global Warming Concerns Continue to Drop," Gallup, www.gallup.com/poll/126560/americans-global-warming-concerns-continue-drop.aspx.

45   **a rise from 35 percent:** Ibid.

45   **a bare majority of 52 percent:** Ibid.

45   **teaching of Scripture:** John M. Broder, "Climate Change Doubt Is Tea Party Article of Faith, *New York Times,* October 20, 2010, www.nytimes.com/2010/10/21/us/politics/21climate.html.

45   **fictitious television ads:** "Polluter-Funded Groups Spending Almost $70 Million on Anti–clean Energy Ads," ThinkProgress, October 22, 2010, http://climateprogress.org/2010/10/22/american-crossroads-the-u-s-chamber-of-commerce-american-crossroads-the-u-s-chamber-of-commerce-american-crossroads-the-u-s-chamber-of-commerce/.

46   **oppose any comprehensive legislation:** Broder, "Climate Change Doubt."

46   **cigar-smoking corporate fat cats:** David W. Chen, "A Favorite Villain in Election Ads: New York City," *New York Times,* October 21, 2010, www.nytimes.com/2010/10/22/nyregion/22ads.html?partner=rss&emc=rss.

46   **hold these banks fully accountable:** "Remarks of President Barack Obama—as Prepared for Delivery, Address to Joint Session of Congress, Tuesday, February 24th, 2009," White House, February 24, 2009, /www.whitehouse.gov/the_press_office/Remarks-of-President-Barack-Obama-Address-to-Joint-Session-of-Congress.

47   **they frankly own the place:** Ryan Grim, "Dick Durbin: Banks 'Frankly Own the Place,'" Huffington Post, April 29, 2009, www.huffingtonpost.com/2009/04/29/dick-durbin-banks-frankly_n_193010.html.

47   **the strongest consumer financial protections:** Jesse Lee, "President Obama Signs Wall Street Reform: 'No Easy Task,'"

White House, July 21, 2010, www.whitehouse.gov/blog/
2010/07/21/president-obama-signs-wall-street-reform-no-easy-task.

47 **excoriated for placing top grades:** Gregory Zuckerman, "Much
Talk, but Little Changed on Wall Street," *Wall Street Journal*,
January 4, 2010, http://online.wsj.com/article/SB10001424052
748704876804574628863431014416.html.

48 **the nation's senior financial authority:** John Cassidy, "The
Volcker Rule," *New Yorker*, July 26, 2010, www.newyorker.com/
reporting/2010/07/26/100726fa_fact_cassidy?currentPage=all.

48 **systemically important banking institutions:** John G. Finley,
"How Financial Reforms Will Impact Private Equity Hedge Funds,"
Harvard Law School Forum on Corporate Governance, June 8,
2010, http://blogs.law.harvard.edu/corpgov/2010/06/08/how-
financial-reforms-will-impact-private-equity-hedge-funds/#4;
www.nytimes.com/2010/06/26/us/politics/26regulate.html?partner
=rss&emc=rss.

48 **a last-minute intervention:** Matt Taibbi, "Wall Street's Big Win,"
Rolling Stone, August 6, 2010, www.rollingstone.com/politics/news/
17390/188551?RS_show_page=0.

48 **a far bigger pool of money:** Ibid.

48 **insurers, mutual funds, and trusts:** Ibid.

49 **trading now be separated out:** Ibid.

49 **client activity as a cover:** Nelson D. Schwartz and Eric Dash,
"Despite Reform, Banks Have Room for Risky Deals," *New York
Times*, August 25, 2010, www.nytimes.com/2010/08/26/
business/economy/26trade.html.

49 **support milk subsidies or sugar tariffs:** Lawrence Lessig,
"Democracy After Citizens United," *Boston Review*, September–
October 2010, www.bostonreview.net?BR35.5/lessig.php.

49 **Consumer Protection Bureau:** Ron Lieber and Tara Siegel
Bernard, "From Card Fees to Mortgages, a New Day for
Consumers," *New York Times*, June 25, 2010,
www.nytimes.com/2010/06/26/your-money/26money.html.

49 **even less regulation:** Ibid.

50 **to foot the bill:** Ross Colvin, "Obama Signs Sweeping Wall Street
Overhaul into Law," Reuters, July 21, 2010, www.reuters.com/
article/idUSTRE66K1QR20100722.

50   **no more taxpayer-funded bailouts:** Ibid.

50   **Congress declined to curb:** Simon Johnson, "The Defanging of Obama's Regulation Plan," *New York Times*, June 18, 2009, http://economix.blogs.nytimes.com/2009/06/18/the-defanging-of-obamas-regulation-plan/.

50   **protect American taxpayers:** Robert Reich, "Does the Obama Plan for Reforming Wall Street Measure Up?" *American Prospect*, June 19, 2009, www.prospect.org/csnc/blogs/tapped_archive ?month=06&year=2009&base_name=does_the_obama_plan _for_reform.

50   **irresponsible investments:** Peter Boone and Simon Johnson, "Way Too Big to Fail," *New Republic*, November 11, 2010, 20–22.

50   **executive pay:** Lieber and Bernard, "From Card Fees to Mortgages."

50   **went home with a bonus of $100 million:** David Segal, "$100 Million Payday Poses Problem for Pay Czar," *New York Times*, August 1, 2009, www.nytimes.com/2009/08/02/business/ 02bonus.html.

50   **record years on Wall Street:** Liz Rappaport, Aaron Luchheyti, and Stephen Grocer, "Wall Street Pay: A Record $144 Million," *Wall Street Journal*, October 11, 2010, http://online.wsj.com/article .SB10001434052738704518104575546542463746562.html.

51   **the share prices of Citigroup:** Christine Hauser, "Banks Likely to Offset Impact of New Law, Analysts Say," *New York Times*, June 25, 2010, www.nytimes.com/2010/06/26/business/26reax.html ?ref=christine_hauser.

51   **triple-digit rise:** Rita Nazareth, "U.S. Stocks Rise as Drug Shares Gain on House Health Bill," Bloomberg, March 22, 2010, www. bloomberg.com/apps/news?pid=newsarchive&sid=a_I5KjWeBKRE.

51   **CNBC's James Cramer:** Jim Cramer, "Cramer: Obamacare Will Topple the Market," The Street, March 16, 2010, www.thestreet.com/story/10703361/cramer-obamacare-will-topple- the-market.html.

51   **banks should be pleased:** "Banks Expected to Offset Impact of Financial Bill," *New York Times: Dealbook*, June 25, 2010, http://dealbook.blogs.nytimes.com/http:// dealbook.blogs.nytimes.com/2010/06/25/some-see-a-tough-law- others-little-change.

51   **insurance companies also mostly dodged:** Jay MacDonald,
     "Insurance Mostly Dodges Financial Reform," Bankrate.com, July
     21, 2010, http://www.bankrate.com/finance/insurance/insurance-
     mostly-dodges-financial-reform-1.aspx.

51   **the complexity of the legislation:** Erich Lichtblau, "Ex-Regulators
     Get Set to Lobby on New Financial Rules," *New York Times*, July
     27, 2010, www.nytimes.com/2010/07/28/business/28lobby.html.

52   **Commodity Futures Trading Commission:** Ibid.

52   **politically sophisticated industry:** Ezra Klein, "Wall Street Rises
     Again," *Washington Post*, September 1, 2010, http://voices
     .washingtonpost.com/ezra-klein/2010/09/wall_street_rises
     _again.html.

52   **148 former regulatory officials:** Summer Lollie, "Ex-Regulators
     Lobby on New Finance Rules, Immigrant Rights Groups Shift
     Focus and More in Capital Eye Opener: July 28," Opensecrets.org,
     July 28, 2010, http://www.opensecrets.org/news/2010/
     07/exregulators-to-lobby-on-new-finance-rules.html.

52   **are written so broadly:** Ibid.

52   **maintain higher fees:** Ibid.

53   **to turn over to the media:** Dennis K. Berman, "Ratings Firms'
     Power Trip Lays Bare Their Weaknesses," *Wall Street Journal*, July
     27, 2010, http://online.wsj.com/article/SB1000
     1424052748704700404575391590543871692.html.

53   **a witches' brew of deregulation:** "'Disappointing and Inspiring':
     Warren, Johnson, Black, and More React to FinReg," Roosevelt
     Institute, July 25, 2010, www.rooseveltinstitute.org/new-
     roosevelt/disappointing-and-inspiring-warren-johnson-black-and
     -more-react-finreg.

54   **according to Public Citizen:** "Revolving Door Spins Quickly
     Between Congress and Wall Street," Public Citizen, June 3, 2010,
     www.citizen.org/pressroom/pressroomredirect.cfm?ID=3141.

54   **a lengthy Huffington Post investigation:** Ryan Grim and Arthur
     Delaney, "The Cash Committee: How Wall Street Wins on the
     Hill," Huffington Post, December 29, 2010, www.huffingtonpost
     .com/2009/12/29/the-cash-committee-how-wa_n_402373.html.

54   **former clients of current committee staff:** Ibid.

55   **a very logical progression:** Ibid.

55   **shift in power:** Mike Madden, "Politico Celebrates Politico,"
       Washington City Paper, November 3, 2010, www.washingtoncity
       paper.com/blogs/citydesk/2010/11/03/politico-celebrates-politico/.

56   **House Minority Leader John Boehner:** Eric Lipton, "A G.O.P.
       Leader Tightly Bound to Lobbyists," *New York Times*, September
       11, 2010, www.nytimes.com/2010/09/12/us/politics/12
       boehner.html?pagewanted=2.

56   **no fewer than forty-five flights:** Ibid.

56   **a premium for Republicans:** Eric Lichtblau, "Lobbyists Rush to
       Hire G.O.P. Staff Ahead of Vote," *New York Times*, September 9,
       2010, www.nytimes.com/2010/09/10/business/10lobby.html.

56   **the new It girl:** Ibid.

56   **ex-staffers-turned-lobbyists earned:** Ryan Grim and Arthur
       Delaney, "On K Street, an Ex-Senate Staffer Is Worth $740,000 a
       Year," Huffington Post, September 24, 2010, www.huffingtonpost
       .com/2010/09/24/post_529_n_738043.html.

56   **I better tell that to my staff:** Ibid.

56   **fewer lobbyists than before:** Jeanne Cummings, "Downturn Has
       Hit Banking Lobbyists," *Politico*, October 19, 2009,
       www.politico.com/news/stories/1009/28439.html.

57   **lobbyists' talking points:** Simon Johnson and James Kwak, "Book:
       Brace for More Financial Woes," MSNBC: Today, April 2, 2010,
       http://today.msnbc.msn.com/id/36083919/ns/today-today_books.

57   **the idea that financial innovation:** Simon Johnson and James
       Kwak, *13 Bankers: The Wall Street Takeover and the Next Financial
       Meltdown* (New York: Pantheon, 2010), 105.

58   **technological change clearly accelerating:** Ibid., 101.

58   **number of Americans living in poverty:** Dennis Cauchon and
       Richard Wolf, "Number of People in Poverty Reaches Highest Level
       in 51 Years," *USA Today*, September 17, 2010,
       www.usatoday.com/news/nation/census/2010-09-16-poverty-rate-
       income-numbers_N.htm.

58   **the poverty line:** Erick Eckholm, "Recession Raises Poverty Rate to
       a 15-Year High," *New York Times*, September 16, 2010,
       www.nytimes.com2010/09/17/us/17poverty.html.

58   **a family of four:** Ibid.
58   **the four hundred richest Americans:** "The Forbes 400,"
      Forbes, September 16, 2010, www.forbes.com/wealth/forbes-
      400?boxes=HomepageSpecialStorySection.
58   **to fund tax breaks:** Beadsie Woo, Ida Rademacher, and Jillien
      Meier, "Upside Down: The $400 Billion Federal Asset-Building
      Budget," Corporation for Enterprise Development and the Annie
      E. Casey Foundation, September 2010. www.aecf.org/Knowledge
      Center/Publications.aspx?pubguid={6D62ACDE-6BAC-4000-
      A356-5185344AFC46.
59   **top 1 percent of taxpayers:** Ibid.
59   **families making $50,000:** Ibid
59   **a degree of political influence:** Johnson and Kwak, *13 Bankers*, 90.
60   **he raised some $240 million:** Eric Lipton and Raymond
      Hernandez, "A Champion of Wall Street Reaps Benefits,"
      New York Times, December 13, 2008,
      www.nytimes.com/2008/12/14/business/14schumer.html.
60   **crazy, anti-business liberals:** Ibid.
60   **embraced the industry's free market:** Ibid.
61   **serving the parochial interest:** Ibid.
61   **a big government liberal:** Jeffrey Toobin, "The Senator and the
      Street," *New Yorker*, August 2, 2010, www.newyorker.com/
      reporting/2010/08/02/100802fa_fact_toobin#ixzz138SfOQuI.
62   **the bill still foundered:** Dan Eggen, "Disclose Act in Jeopardy
      After Interest Groups Balk at NRA Deal," *Washington Post*, June 18,
      2010, www.washingtonpost.com/wp-
      dyn/content/article/2010/06/17/AR2010061705859.html.
62   **a September 2010 vote on the bill:** Ben Smith, "Disclose Vote
      Will Wait for High-Dollar Fundraiser," *Politico*, September 21,
      2010, www.politico.com/blogs/bensmith/0910/DISCLOSE
      _vote_will_wait_for_highdollar_fundraiser.html.
62   **Federal Election Commission:** Jesse Zwick, "Except in the
      Narrowest Circumstances, FEC Won't Enforce Disclosure
      Requirements," *Washington Independent*, August 201, 2010,
      http://washingtonindependent.com/95395/except-in-the-
      narrowest-circumstances-fec-wont-enforce-disclosure-requirements.

62   **a three-billion-dollar weathervane:** Mayer, "Covert Operations."

62   **when Obama was strong:** Ibid.

63   **the country's largest business lobby:** Jim Kuhnhenn, "Chamber Emerges as Formidable Political Force," Associated Press, August 21, 2010, www.msnbc.msn.com/id/38797920/39619593.

63   **an art form:** Eric Lipton, Mike McIntire and Don Van Natta Jr., "Top Companies Aid Chamber of Commerce in Policy Fights," *New York Times*, October 21, 2010.

63   **Bush political guru Karl Rove:** Dan Eggen, "Campaign Watchdogs Accuse Top Conservative Group of Violating Tax Laws," *Washington Post*, October 5, 2010, www.washingtonpost.com/wp-dyn/content/article/2010/10/05/AR2010100501790.html.

63   **one incomplete list:** Justin Elliot, "Billionaires Give 91 Percent of Funds for Rove-Tied Group," Salon, September 20, 2010, www.salon.com/news/politics/war_room/2010/09/20/rove_group_more_millionaire_donations.

63   **gave $7 million alone:** Jeanne Cummings, "Texas Builder Gives Crossroads $7M," *Politico*, October 20, 2010, http://dyn.politico.com/printstory.cfm?uuid=CC46CD96-E6AD-7212-6ADCDA8E37D285CA.

64   **refuses to identify:** See Matt Corley, "'Jew Counter' Fred Malek Now Counting Republican Minority Candidates," ThinkProgress, June 8, 2010, http://thinkprogress.org/2010/06/08/malek-count-minorities/; and George Zornick, "'Unethical' Nixon Campaign Vet Fred Malek Still Dodging Campaign Fanance Laws," Thinkprogress, October 18, 2010, http://thinkprogress.org/2010/10/18/malek-campaign-fundraising/.

64   **Republican candidates outspent:** Kristen Jensen and Jonathan Salen, "Republican-Leaning Groups Outspend Democratic Counterparts 7–1 This Month," Bloomberg, September 23, 2010, www.bloomberg.com/news/2010-09-23/republican-leaning-groups-outspend-democratic-counterparts-7-1-this-month.html.

64   **the appearance of corruption:** E. J. Dionne Jr., "Shadowy Players in a New Class War," *Washington Post*, October 11, 2010, www.washingtonpost.com/wp-dyn/content/article/2010/10/10/AR2010101003045.html.

64   **Government has a compelling interest:** David G. Savage,
     "Question of Foreign Funding of U.S. Elections Unsettled," *Los
     Angeles Times*, January 31, 2010, http://articles.latimes.com/2010/
     jan/31/nation/la-na-election-rules31-2010jan31.

65   **roughly $400 million:** Scott Keyes, "Report: Conservative Groups
     Gearing Up to Spend $400 Million on Midterm Election,"
     ThinkProgress, August 27, 2010, http://thinkprogress.org/2010/
     08/27/conservative-groups-400-millio.

65   **as inconsequential in your life:** Jeff Zeleny, "Republicans
     Weighing Party's Message," *New York Times*, April 9, 2010,
     www.nytimes.com/2010/04/10/us/politics/10memo.html.

66   **Americans questioned trusted:** Liz Halloran, "Pew Poll: Trust in
     Government Hits Near-Historic Low," NPR, August 18, 2010,
     www.npr.org/templates/story/story.php?storId=126047343.

66   **Koch Family Foundation:** Mayer, "Covert Operations."

66   **Mercatus Center:** "About," Mercatus Center at George Mason
     University, http://mercatus.org/about.

67   **freedom in economic arrangements:** Milton Friedman, *Capitalism
     and Freedom* (Chicago: University of Chicago Press, 1962),
     www.mtholyoke.edu/acad/intrel/ipe/friedman.html.

67   **the philosophy of freedom:** Jonathan Chait, "Fact Finders," *New
     Republic*, February 28, 2005, www.tnr.com/article/politics/
     fact-finders.

67   **markets are voting machines:** Kevin Phillips, *Wealth and
     Democracy: A Political History of the American Rich* (New York:
     Broadway, 2003), 338.

68   **the mantle of Milton Friedman:** Sewell Chan, "Friedman Casts
     Shadow as Economists Meet," *New York Times*, November 7, 2010,
     www.newyorktimes.com/2010/11/08/business/economy/08fed.htm
     l?_r=1&ref=federal_reserve_system.

68   **its political possibilities:** Irving Kristol, *Neoconservatism: The
     Autobiography of an Idea* (New York: Free Press, 1995), 338.

68   **fundamental assumptions of contemporary liberalism:** Ibid.,
     485.

68   **supply-side economics:** Martin Wolf, "The Political Genius of
     Supply-Side Economics," *Financial Times*, July 25, 2010,

http://blogs.ft.com/martin-wolf-exchange/2010/07/25/the-political-genius-of-supply-side-economics.

70   **government is going to monitor:** Goodell, "As the World Burns."
70   **all chiefs and no Indians:** Mayer, "Covert Operations."
70   **inhibit** Ibid.
71   **cokehead in chief:** Ibid.
71   **demonic possession:** Ibid.
71   **train Tea Party organizers:** Ibid.
71   **socialist vision for this country:** Ibid.
71   **a rented UPS mailbox:** Jason Hancock, "Secrets of the American Future Fund," *Iowa Independent*, August 19, 2008, http://iowaindependent.com/4203/secrets-of-the-american-future-fund.
71   **a conservative and free market viewpoint:** "About Us," American Future Fund, http://americanfuturefund.com/about-us.
71   **receives significant funding:** Jesse Zwick, "Bruce Rastetter, the Original Money Behind American Future Fund," *Iowa Independent*, October 10, 2010, http://iowaindependent.com/45073/bruce-rastetter-the-original-money-behind-american-future-fund.
72   **interests of the ethanol industry:** Jim Rutenberg, Don Van Natta Jr., and Mike McIntire, "Offering Donors Secrecy, and Going on Attack," *New York Times*, October 11, 2010, www.nytimes.com/2010/10/12/us/politics/12donate.html.
72   **owner of the Chicago Cubs:** Amanda Turkel, "The One-Person Funded Super PAC: How Wealthy Donors Can Skirt Campaign Finance Restrictions," Huffington Post, October 22, 2010, www.huffingtonpost.com/2010/10/21/super-pac-taxpayers-earmarks-concerned-citizens-campaign-finance_n_772214.html.
72   **grassroots citizens' movement:** Rutenberg, Van Natta, and McIntire, "Offering Donors Secrecy."

CHAPTER FIVE

73   **television has made an enormous impact:** Pete Hamill, "The Revolt of the White Lower Middle Class," *New York Magazine*, April 14, 1969.
74   **doubled the viewership:** Brian Stelter, "For Fox News, Most Viewers Ever for a Midterm Election," *New York Times*,

November 3, 2010, http://mediadecoder.blogs.nytimes.com/2010/11/03/for-fox-news-most-viewers-ever-for-a-midterm-election/.

74   **a cyclonic, perpetual emotion machine:** Quoted in Chris Smith, "America Is a Joke: The Worst of Times for Politics and Media Has Been the Best of Times for The Daily Show's Host–and Unfortunately Things Are Getting Even Funnier," *New York Magazine*. September 12, 2010, http://nymag.com/arts/tv/profiles/68086/.

74   **half a billion dollars:** Amanda Turkel, "The One-Person Funded Super PAC: How Wealthy Donors Can Skirt Campaign Finance Restrictions," Huffington Post, October 22, 2010, www.huffingtonpost.com/2010/10/21/super-pac-taxpayers-earmarks-concerned-citizens-campaign-finance_n_772214.html.

75   **Republicans originally thought:** Quoted, among other places, in Eric Alterman, "Think Again: Just What Exactly Is Fox News?" Center for American Progress, October 7, 2010, www.americanprogress.org/issues/2010/10/ta100710.html.

75   **Mitt Romney:** Jonathan Martin and Keach Hagey, "Fox Primary: Complicated, Contractual," *Politico*, September 27, 2010, www.politico.com/news/stories/0910/42745.html.

75   **he had to first get Fox's permission:** Quoted, among other places, in Alterman, "Think Again."

76   **to book many of them:** Quoted in Ben Smith, "The Fox Primary," *Politico*, September 27, 2010, www.politico.com/blogs/bensmith/0910/The_Fox_primary.html.

76   **offer their views:** Martin and Hagey, "Fox Primary."

76   **the cold reality is:** Ibid.

76   **go with her gut:** Quoted, among other places, in Eric Lach, "Palin Counsels Christine O'Donnell: 'Speak Through Fox News' (VIDEO)," TPM, September 16, 2010, http://tpmdc.talkingpointsmemo.com/2010/09/palin-counsels-christine-odonnell-speak-through-fox-news-video.php.

77   **sad and pathetic people:** Karl Rove, interviewed by Alisyn Camerota, "Rove: Fox News 'Sad' for Using Old Material," *Politico*, April 18, 2010,

http://videoshare.politico.com/singletitlevideo.php?bcpid=1940722
4001&bctid=78708102001.

77 **already a prominent presence:** Jim Rutenberg, "Rove Returns,
with Team, Planning G.O.P. Push," *New York Times*, September 25,
2010, www.nytimes.com/2010/09/26/us/26rove.html?
_r=2&ref=karl_rove.

77 **an anti-Democratic barrage of attack ads:** Ibid.

77 **lose a big game:** Ibid.

78 **I'm really reaching out:** Eric Hananoki, "Sharron Angle Brags
About Her Fundraising from 'friendly' Outlets Like Fox News,"
County Fair, September 22, 2010, http://mediamatters.org/blog/
201009220018.

78 **Angle added, in an interview:** Sharron Angle, interviewed by Carl
Camercon, quoted, among other places, in Matt DeLong, "Sharron
Angle: Press Should 'Ask the Questions We Want to Answer,'"
Washington Post, August 3, 2010, http://voices.washingtonpost
.com/44/2010/08/sharron-angle-press-should-ask.html.

78 **twenty Fox News personalities:** "Report: Fox Newsers Rally for
GOP in More Than 300 Instances and in Every State," Media
Matters, April 21, 2010, http://mediamatters.org/research/
201004210012.

78 **without Fox News:** Martin and Hagey, "Fox Primary."

79 **gave a $1.25 million donation:** Ben Smith, "News Corp. Gave
$1 million to Pro-GOP group," *Politico*, September 30, 2010,
www.politico.com/news/stories/0910/42989.html; Lee Fang, "Rupert
Murdoch's News Corporation Donates Again to the Republican
Governors Association: $250,000," ThinkProgress, October 15, 2010,
http://thinkprogress.org/2010/10/15/news-corp-republican.

79 **during the first quarter of 2010:** Dylan Stableford, "Driven by Fox
News, News Corp. Sees 8% Profit Growth," *The Wrap*, November
4, 2010, www.thewrap.com/media/column-post/news-corp-glee-
fox-news-murdoch-earnings-22247.

79 **Obama's green czar resigns:** Eric Alterman, "Just Don't Call It
'Journalism,'" *The Nation*, October 21, 2009,
www.thenation.com/article/just-dont-call-it-journalism.

80   **advancing a secret agenda:** "Why Republican Leaders Will Have Trouble Speaking to the Rest of America," Democracy Corps, October 16, 2009, www.democracycorps.com/focus/2009/10/the-very-separate-world-of-conservative-republicans/?section=Analysis.

80   **a straight-out lie:** E. J. Dionne Jr., "Enough Right-Wing Propaganda," *Washington Post*, July 26, 2010, www.washingtonpost.com/wp-dyn/content/article/2010/07/25/AR2010072502756.html. NBC poll is also available at http://msnbcmedia.msn.com/i/MSNBC/Sections/NEWS/NBC-WSJ_Poll.pdf.

80   **the second they focus on us:** Ryan Lizza, "As the World Burns: How the Senate and the White House Missed Their Best Chance to Deal with Climate Change," *New Yorker*, October 11, 2010, www.newyorker.com/reporting/2010/10/11/101011fa_fact_lizza?printable=true#ixzz132SmbCSo.

81   **fully 60 percent:** "Growing Number of Americans Say Obama Is a Muslim: Religion, Politics, and the President," Pew Forum on Religion and Public Life, August 18, 2010, http://pewforum.org/Politics-and-Elections/Growing-Number-of-Americans-Say-Obama-is-a-Muslim.aspx.

81   **no friend to America:** Bill O'Reilly, "O'Reilly Factor Flash," August 18, 2010, www.billoreilly.com/show?action=viewTVShow&showID=2672#1.

81   **Glenn Beck falsely claimed:** "Beck Smears Rauf with Falsehoods, Innuendo, and Hypocrisy," Media Matters, August 11, 2010, http://mediamatters.org/research/201008110039.

81   **Sean Hannity claimed:** "Hannity Falsely Claims Imam Rauf Wants to 'Shred Our Constitution,'" Media Matters, August 13, 2010, http://mediamatters.org/research/201008130002.

82   **Islam's original values:** Feisal Abdul Rauf, *What's Right with Islam: A New Vision for Muslims and the West* (New York: Harper Collins, 2004).

82   **Fox's hosts drove themselves:** Faiz Shakir, "Fox Shareholder Prince Alwaleed Meets with News Corp Execs to Discuss How to 'Strengthen the Alliance,'" ThinkProgress, August 24, 2010, http://thinkprogress.org/2010/08/24/fox-stewart-alwaleed; Charlie

Rose, "Charlie Rose: A Q&A with Prince Alalweed bin Talal: The Saudi Prince on Citigroup, News Corp., Obama, Taxes, and Terrorism," *Business Week*, January 21, 2010, www.businessweek .com/magazine/content/10_05/b4165010350026.htm.

82   **and he funds this imam:** Steve Benen, "Political Animal," Washington Monthly, August 24, 2010, www.washingtonmonthly .com/archives/individual/2010_08/025354.php.

82   **bin Talal:** Tim Arango, "Fox News Insinuates, but Investor Shrugs It Off," *New York Times*, October 17, 2010, www.nytimes.com/ 2010/10/18/business/media/18prince.html?scp=4&sq=%22nothing %20to%20do%22%20Park51,%20&st=cse.

82   **a record number of Muslim workers:** Steven Greenhouse, "Muslims Report Rising Discrimination at Work," *New York Times*, September 23, 2010, www.nytimes.com/2010/09/24/business/ 24muslim.html.

83   **Sharron Angle complained:** Cristina Silva, "Nevada Senate Hopeful Sharron Angle: Muslim Law Takes Hold in Dearborn, Other U.S. Cities," *Detroit Free Press*, October 8, 2010, www.freep.com/article/20101008/NEWS07/101008018/1318/ Senate-hopeful-Muslim-law-is-taking-over-Dearborn-other-cities#ixzz135qmPtkM; Reza Aslan, "America's Sharia Hysteria," *Daily Beast*, October 12, 2010, www.thedailybeast.com/blogs-and-stories/2010-10-12/sharron-angle-and-the-anti-muslim-scare-about-sharia-law-in-america.

83   **the Pew Project on Excellence in Journalism:** "State of the News Media: An Annual Report on American Journalism, 2009," Pew Project for Excellence in Journalism, www.stateofthemedia.org/2009/about_the_study.php?media=13.

83   **most radical president ever:** Rush Limbaugh, "Obama Performs Statist-Assisted Suicide on the American Economy," *Rush Limbaugh Show*, April 8, 2010, www.rushlimbaugh.com/home/daily/site_ 040810/content/01125106.guest.html.

84   **a deep-seated hatred for white people:** Glenn Beck, quoted in "Beck: Obama Has 'Exposed Himself as a Guy' with 'a Deep-Seated Hatred for White People,'" Media Matters, July 28, 2009, http://mediamatters.org/mmtv/200907280008.

84   **represent a consensus:** Rupert Murdoch, quoted in "Murdoch:
     Glenn Beck Was 'Right' to Say Obama Is 'a Racist' with 'a Deep-
     Seated Hatred for White People,'" ThinkProgress, November 9,
     2009, http://thinkprogress.org/2009/11/09/murdoch-beck-right.

84   **Beck feels no compunction:** Glenn Beck, quoted in Jeremy
     Holden, "Glenn Beck's Sua Culpa," Media Matters, August 2, 2010,
     http://mediamatters.org/blog/201008020066; Glenn Beck, quoted
     in Joan Flash, "'It's Like the Damn Planet of the Apes!'" Salon,
     August 6, 2010, www.salon.com/news/opinion/joan_walsh/
     politics/2010/08/06/glenn_beck_planet_of_the_apes.

84   **a 1936 book:** Glenn Beck, quoted in "Glenn Beck Promotes Book
     Rife with Anti-Semitism and Racism," Media Matters, June 4,
     2010, http://mediamatters.org/research/201006070053.

85   **a nice little chicken dinner:** Steven Thrasher, "White America Has
     Lost Its Mind," *Village Voice* online edition, September 29, 2010,
     www.villagevoice.com/2010-09-29/news/white-america-has-lost-its-
     mind.

85   **Fox TV host Laura Ingraham:** Laura Ingraham, *The Obama
     Diaries* (New York: Simon and Schuster, 2010) 88, 101.

85   **a larger, nefarious cabal:** Eric Boehlert, "Beck's Incendiary Angst Is
     Dangerously Close to Having a Body Count," Media Matters, July
     27, 2010, http://mediamatters.org/blog/201007270004.

85   **staffed by thugs:** Ibid.

85   **Byron Williams:** Henry K. Lee, "Alleged Gunman Says He Wanted
     'a Revolution,'" *San Francisco Chronicle*, July 21, 2010,
     http://articles.sfgate.com/2010-07-21/news/21991372_1
     _chp-officers-body-armor-san-francisco.

85   **railroading through all these left-wing agenda:** Bob Egelko and
     Henry K. Lee, "I-580 Shootout Suspect Mad at Left-Wing Politics;
     Parolee in Body Armor Injured, 2 Officers Hurt" *San Francisco
     Chronicle*, July 19, 2010, http://articles.sfgate.com/2010-07-19/bay-
     area/21988908_1_chp-officers-bullet-resistant-vest-williams-mother.

85   **in a jailhouse interview:** Dana Milbank, "Conspiracy Theorists
     Find Validation from Glenn Beck," *Washington Post* online edition,
     October 10, 2010, www.washingtonpost.com/wp-dyn/content/
     article/2010/10/08/AR2010100805640.html.

86   **Williams opened fire:** Boehlert, "Beck's Incendiary Angst."

86   **Obama is pushing America:** Glenn Beck, quoted in "Beck Suggests Obama Is 'Trying to Destroy the Country' and Is Pushing America Toward Civil War," Media Matters, May 19, 2010, http://mediamatters.org/mmtv/201005190026.

86   **violent fear-mongering:** Glenn Beck, quoted in "Beck Caps Two Weeks of Violent Fear Mongering About Progressives by Warning That Eventually "They Just Start Shooting People," Media Matters, May 27, 2010, http://mediamatters.org/blog/201005270029.

86   **people around the president support:** Glenn Beck, quoted in "Beck: "'The People Around the President' Thought About and Plotted 'Armed Insurrection' and 'Bombing,'" Media Matters, March 24, 2010, http://mediamatters.org/mmtv/201003240055.

86   **Obama administration will kill him:** Glenn Beck, quoted in "Mixed Message: Beck Spews Violent Rhetoric, but Tells Audience to Reject Violence," Media Matters, July 27, 2010, http://mediamatters.org/research/201007270045.

86   **a quote from Thomas Jefferson:** Glenn Beck, quoted in "After Quoting Jefferson, Beck Says, "There Will Be Rivers of Blood If We Don't Have Values and Principles," Media Matters, May 14, 2010, http://mediamatters.org/mmtv/201005140063.

86   **compared himself to Israeli Nazi hunters:** Glenn Beck, quoted in "Beck Likens Himself to 'Israeli Nazi Hunters': 'To the Day I Die, I Am Going to Be a Progressive Hunter,'" Media Matters, January 20, 2010, http://mediamatters.org/mmtv/201001200016.

86   **advice to Liberty University grads:** Glenn Beck, quoted in "Beck's Advice to His Daughter, Liberty U Grads, Includes 'Shoot to Kill,'" Media Matters May 15, 2010, http://mediamatters.org/mmtv/201005150019; Glenn Beck, quoted in "Beck at Liberty U: We All "Have a Responsibility' to Speak About 'What Time It Is' or 'Blood . . . Will Be on Our Hands,'" Media Matters, May 15, 2010, http://mediamatters.org/mmtv/201005150016.

86   **world is on edge:** Glenn Beck, quoted in "Beck Says 'Those Who Survive' Will 'Stand in the Truth,' 'Listen,' 'Watch,'" Media Matters, May 25, 2010, http://mediamatters.org/mmtv/201005250064.

86   **blood in the streets:** Glenn Beck, quoted in "Beck Says Some
      Progressive Groups Don't Have 'a Problem with Blood in the
      Streets,'" Media Matters, June 09, 2010, http://mediamatters.org
      /mmtv/201006090056.

86   **eating rock soup:** Glenn Beck, quoted in "Beck: Present Day Will
      Seem Like Good Times 'When We're Behind Barbed Wire and Just
      Eating Rock Soup,'" Media Matters, July 30, 2010,
      http://mediamatters.org/mmtv/201007300006.

87   **a symphony of anti-Semitic dog-whistles:** Michelle Goldberg,
      "Glen Beck's anti-Semitic Attacks," *Daily Beast*, November 11,
      2010, www.thedailybeast.com/blogs-and-stories/2010-11-10/
      glenn-becks-anti-semitic-attack-on-george-soros/, and Brian
      Stelter, "Glenn Beck's Attacks on George Soros Draw Heat,"
      New York Times, November 11, 2010, www.nytimes.com/
      2010/11/12/us/12beck.html?_r=1&scp=1&sp=beck
      ,%20soros&st=cse.

87   **the Tea Party Express:** "'Party on!' Fox Relentlessly Promotes
      Tea Party Express Tour," Media Matters, October 19, 2010,
      http://mediamatters.org/mobile/research/201010190022.

88   **bus tour that took the country by storm:** Ibid.

88   **We Colored People:** "Fox's Tea Party Affiliate Expelled from
      National Tea Party Federation," Media Matters, July 19, 2010,
      http://mediamatters.org/research/201007190044.

90   **had interpreted the election:** Fouad Ajami, "The Obama Spell Is
      Broken, Unlike This President, John Kennedy Was an Ironist Who
      Never Fell for His Own Mystique," *Wall Street Journal*, February 2,
      2010, http://online.wsj.com/article/SB1000142405274870
      40943045750291101104772360.html.

90   **another anti-Obama op-ed:** Dorothy Rabinowitz, "The Alien in
      the White House: The Distance Between the President and the
      People Is Beginning to Be Revealed," *Wall Street Journal*, June 9,
      2010, http://online.wsj.com/article/SB100014240527487033026
      04575294231631318728.html.

90   **the most self-punishing person:** Peggy Noonan, "America Is at
      Risk of Boiling Over: And Out-of-Touch Leaders Don't See the
      Need to Cool Things Off," *Wall Street Journal*, August 7, 2010,

http://online.wsj.com/article/SB10001424052738703748904575411713335505250.html.

90   **to cite just one statistic:** *Economic Report of the President,* 2006, www.gpoaccess.gov/eop/2006/2006_erp.pdf.

91   **federal government continues its standoff:** Noonan, "America Is at Risk."

91   **authorities deported 392,862 people:** Julia Preston, "Deportations from U.S. Hit a Record High," *New York Times,* October 6, 2010, www.nytimes.com/2010/10/07/us/07immig.html.

91   **after Noonan's column appeared:** Phil Leggiere, "Secure Communities Expanded," *Homeland Security Today,* August 13, 2010, http://www.hstoday.us/content/view/14317/149.

92   **a net outflow:** Jeffrey Passel and D'Vera Cohn, "U.S. Unauthorized Immigration Flows Are Down Sharply Since Mid-Decade," Pew Hispanic Center, September 1, 2010, http://pewhispanic.org/reports/report.php?ReportID=126.

92   **Arizona would impose:** Randal C. Archibold, "Judge Blocks Arizona's Immigration Law," *New York Times,* July 28, 2010, www.nytimes.com/2010/07/29/us/29arizona.html.

92   **a sign of Democratic panic:** Peggy Noonan, "Try a Little Tenderness: Chris Christie, not the Tea Party, Is the Model for the Republicans," *Wall Street Journal,* July 30, 2010, http://online.wsj.com/article/SB10001424052748703578104575397671235195094.html.

92   **the need for a wise man:** Peggy Noonan, "Youth Has Outlived Its Usefulness: American Politics Is Desperately in Need of Adult Supervision," *Wall Street Journal,* July 16, 2010, http://online.wsj.com/article/SB10001424052748704682604575369513252243689.html.

92   **rampant lesbianism:** "Meet the Knuckleheads of the U.S. Senate: The Senate Has Come a Long Way Since Ted Kennedy Arrived in Washington In 1962. But Not in the Right Direction," Salon, September 8, 2010, www.salon.com/news/feature/2009/09/08/knuckleheads/index1.html.

93   **exercising his wisdom:** Gardiner Harris, "Senate Bill on Food Safety Is Stalled," *New York Times,* September 18, 2010, www.nytimes.com/2010/09/19/health/policy/19food.html.

93   **the story of the dolphins:** Peggy Noonan, "Why Did They Do It?"
      Wall Street Journal, April 24, 2000,
      www.opinionjournal.com/columnists/pnoonan/?id=95000429.

94   **review by James K. Glassman:** James K. Glassman, "Subsidy as a
      Way of Life: In the U.S. It's 'Work, Work, Work.' A Rock
      Drummer in France Gets a State Stipend," *Wall Street Journal*,
      August 16, 2010, http://online.wsj.com/article/SB100014240
      52748703960004575427731291231298.html.

94   **a wide gap has opened up:** Ibid.

94   **European model is flat-out unsustainable:** Jonathan Cohn,
      "Neoliberal Utopia Awaits," *New Republic*, January 1, 2006,
      www.tnr.com/article/neoliberal-utopia-awaits.

94   **these same European nations:** Organization for Economic
      Cooperation and Development data cited in Lawrence Mitchell,
      Jared Bernstein, and John Schmitt, *The State of Working America,
      2000–2001* (Ithaca, NY: Cornell University Press, 2001), 373.

95   **Finland was number one:** "The World's Best Countries,"
      Newsweek, August 20, 2010, www.newsweek.com/2010/08/15/
      interactive-infographic-of-the-worlds-best-countries.html.

95   **yet 24.7 percent of the elderly:** Thomas Geoghegan, *Were You
      Born on the Wrong Continent?: How the European Model Can Help
      You Get a Life* (New York: Free Press, 2010) 7.

95   **Glassman's bio:** Glassman, "Subsidy as a Way of Life."

95   **the Dow Jones average:** Dow Jones Industrial Average, Yahoo
      Finance, October 2010, http://finance.yahoo.com/q/hp?s=^DJI
      +Historical+Prices.

96   **the transformed political landscape:** "A New Presidency: How
      Bush Should Spend His Windfall of Political Capital," *Wall Street
      Journal*, September 19, 2001.

96   **a terrible thing to exploit:** "The Message of Massachusetts: A
      Crisis Is a Terrible Thing to Exploit," *Wall Street Journal*, January
      19, 2010, http://online.wsj.com/article/SB1000142405274870
      4541004575011021604106924.html.

96   **critic David Zurawik:** David Zurawik, "White House War on Fox:
      Echoes of Nixon-Agnew," *Baltimore Sun*, October 12, 2010,

http://weblogs.baltimoresun.com/entertainment/zontv/2009/10/fox
_news_channel_anita_dunn_ba.html.

98   **Jake Tapper complained:** Jake Tapper and Robert Gibbs, "Political
Punch: Power, Pop, and Probings from ABC News Senior White
House Correspondent Jake Tapper," http://blogs.abcnews.com/
politicalpunch/2009/10/todays-qs-for-os-wh-10202009.html.

98   **it's pushing a point of view:** George Stephanopoulos, "Axelrod: Fox
News Is 'Not Really a News Organization,'" George's Bottom Line,
ABC News, October 18, 2009, http://blogs.abcnews.com/george/
2009/10/axelrod-fox-news-is-not-really-a-news-organization.html.

99   **racist birther Lou Dobbs:** "Meet Erick Erickson: CNN's Newest
Political Commentator," Media Matters, March 16, 2010,
http://mediamatters.org/research/201003160037.

99   **cohost Mika Brzezinski:** "Brzezinski: Palin's Views Connect with
'Real Americans,'" Media Matters, July 06, 2009,
http://mediamatters.org/mmtv/200907060002.

99   **CNBC's Jim Cramer:** Eric Boehlert, "Paging CNBC's Jim Cramer:
Where's the "Gigantic" Scott Brown Stock Market Rally?" Media
Matters, January 20, 2010, http://mediamatters.org/blog/
201001200021.

99   **this philandering, inebriated African socialist:** Dinesh D'Souza,
quoted in Maureen Dowd, "Who's the Con Man?" *New York Times,*
September 14, 2010, www.nytimes.com/2010/09/15/opinion/
15dowd.html.

100 **the *Washington Post*'s op-ed page:** Heather MacDonald, "Dinesh
D'Souza's Poison," Secular Right, September 27, 2010,
http://secularright.org/SR/wordpress/?p=4815.

100 **played a wonderful con:** Alex Pareene, "Newt Gingrich on Obama the
"Kenyan Anti-colonial" Con Man: The Former Speaker of the House
Explains That the President Hates America Because of His African
Socialist Father," Salon, September 13, 2010, www.salon.com/news/
politics/war_room/2010/09/13/newt_dsouza_obama_kenyan_con.

100 **ACORN boasted field offices:** Harold Meyerson, "Acorn's Fall,"
The American Prospect online, November 8, 2010,
http://prospect.org/cs/articles?article=acorns_fall.

101   **in the case of ACORN:** Clark Hoyt, "The Acorn Sting Revisited,"
        New York Times, March 20, 2010, www.nytimes.com/2010/03/
        21/opinion/21pubed.html.
101   **long after the damage:** Ibid.
102   **our vindication:** Michael Hirshhorn, "Truth Lies Here," *Atlantic
        Monthly,* November 2010, www.theatlantic.com/magazine/archive/
        2010/11/truth-lies-here/8246.
102   **many in the conservative media:** "Brown Releases Report
        Detailing a Litany of Problems with ACORN, but No Criminality,"
        Office of the Attorney General, April 1, 2010,
        http://ag.ca.gov/newsalerts/release.php?id=1888; Charles J. Hynes,
        "Kings County District Attorney Charles J. Hynes Makes
        Statement Regarding Investigation into Acorn," Kings County
        District Attorney Office, March 1, 2010, www.brooklynda.org/
        press_releases/pr_mar_10.htm#01.
103   **the paper's ombudsman, Andrew Alexander:**
        "'Liberal Bias' Myth Lives On," Media Matters, September 20,
        2009, http://mediamatters.org/blog/200909200013.
103   **managing editor Jill Abramson:** Clark Hoyt, "Tuning in Too
        Late," *New York Times,* September 26, 2009, www.nytimes.com/
        2009/09/27/opinion/27pubed.html.
103   **not the biggest issue:** George Stephanopoulos, "Obama on
        ACORN: 'Not Something I've Followed Closely,' Won't Commit to
        Cut Federal Funds," *ABC News,* September 20, 2009, http://
        blogs.abcnews.com/george/2009/09/obama-on-acorn-not-
        something-ive-followed-closely.html.
104   **the agenda-setting effect:** Peter Dreier and Christopher Martin,
        "Manipulating the Public Agenda: Why ACORN Was in the News,
        and What the News Got Wrong," UEPI, September 23, 2009,
        http://departments.oxy.edu/uepi/acornstudy.
104   **the only story frame:** Ibid.
104   **on the verge of maybe penetrating:** Meyerson, "Acorn's Fall."
105   **Rove played a central role:** Ibid.
106   **ACORN had stolen the 2008 election:** Ibid.
106   **forced its propaganda:** Dionne, "Enough Right-Wing
        Propaganda."

106 **Secretary of Agriculture Tom Vilsack:** Ben Smith, "Official: No White House Pressure on Sherrod," *Politico*, July 20, 2010, www.politico.com/blogs/bensmith/0710/Official_No_White_House_pressure_on_Sherrod.html.

106 **Deputy Undersecretary Cheryl Cook:** Ed O'Keefe and Krissah Thompson, "NAACP, White House Respond to Ouster of USDA Worker Shirley Sherrod," *Washington Post*, July 20, 2010, http://voices.washingtonpost.com/federal-eye/2010/07/usda_worker_quits_over_racism.html.

107 **he was caught attempting:** "FBI Arrests James O'Keefe at Landrieu's Office," *Atlantic Monthly*, January 26, 2010, http://www.theatlantic.com/politics/archive/2010/01/fbi-arrests-james-okeefe-at-landrieus-office/34243/.

108 **folks at Politico appear:** Meteor Blades, "Sunday Snooze Talk: The Skewpot," Daily Kos, May 9, 2010, www.dailykos.com/storyonly/2010/5/9/864977/-Sunday-Snooze-Talk:-The-Skewpot.

108 **Paul Krugman:** Ibid.

108 **left-leaning think tanks:** Steve Rendall and Michael Morel, "Does NewsHour 'Help Us See America Whole'?" *Extra*, November–December 2010, www.fair.org/index.php?page=4177&printer_friendly=1.

109 **protecting the rights of terrorists:** "Gingrich: Obama Cares More About 'Protecting the Rights of Terrorists' Than the 'Lives of Americans,'" ThinkProgress, December 30, 2009, http://thinkprogress.org/2009/12/30/gingrich-terrorist-rights.

109 **we had no domestic attacks:** Rachel Weiner, "Rudy Giuliani: 'We Had No Domestic Attacks Under Bush; We've Had One Under Obama,'" Huffington Post, January 8, 2010, www.huffington post.com/2010/01/08/rudy-giuliani-we-had-no-d_n_416033.html.

110 **his body language:** "President Obama Owns Ed Henry: 'I Like to Know What I'm Talking About Before I Speak,'" Daily Kos TV, March 24, 2009, www.dailykos.com/tv/w/001049.

110 **can you describe it?:** Maureen Dowd, "A Storyteller Loses the Story Line," *New York Times*, June 1, 2010, www.nytimes.com/2010/06/02/opinion/02dowd.html.

III   **Mark Liebovich notes:** Mark Liebovich, "The Man the White
      House Wakes Up To," *New York Times*, April 21, 2010,
      www.nytimes.com/2010/04/25/magazine/25allen-t.html?page
      wanted=all.

III   **every worst trend in reporting:** Mark Salter, quoted in George
      Packer, "Mike Allen and Nay Phone Latt," *New Yorker* blog, April
      27, 2010, www.newyorker.com/online/blogs/
      georgepacker/2010/04/mike-allen-nay-phone-latt.htlm.

II2   **Balloon Boy story:** Mark Jurkowitz, "Balloon Boy Takes Media for
      a Ride: Snow Day Puts Health Care News Atop Media Agenda,"
      Pew Research Center, October 20, 2009,
      http://pewresearch.org/pubs/1384/media-coverage-of-balloon-boy.

II2   **she received 50 percent more coverage:** Michael Calderone, "The
      Most Covered Candidate of 2010: Christine O'Donnell," *The
      Upshot*, November 2, 2010, http://news.yahoo.com/s/yblog
      _upshot/20101102/el_yblog_upshot/odonnell-receives-most-
      coverage-of-2010-candidates.

II3   **for sheer idiocy:** "Conservatives Continue to Use Fox's *24* to
      Support Hawkish Policies," Media Matters, February 02, 2007,
      http://mediamatters.org/research/200702020015.

II3   **Domenech later defended himself:** Ben Domenech, "The White
      House, Elena Kagan, and Me," Huffington Post, April 16, 2010,
      www.huffingtonpost.com/ben-domenech/the-white-house-
      elena-kag_b_540633.html.

II4   **admitted liar, video-doctor:** Matt Gertz, "Failing Upward: Breitbart
      to Be Featured in ABC's Election Coverage," Media Matters,
      October 29, 2010, http://mediamatters.org/blog/201010290035.

II4   **forced to forfeit:** Michael Calderone, "ABC News Cuts Ties with
      Breitbart on Election Day," *The Upshot*, November 2, 2010,
      http://news.yahoo.com/s/yblog_upshot/20101102/cm_yblog_upsh
      ot/abc-news-cuts-ties-with-breitbart-on-election-day.

II4   **committed to the destruction:** Jay Rosen, "'I'm Committed
      to the Destruction of the Old Media Guard': ABC News and
      Andrew Breitbart," *Pressthink*, November 3, 2010,
      http://pressthink.org/2010/11/im-committed-to-the-destruction-of-
      the-old-media-guard-abc-news-and-andrew-breitbart/.

CONCLUSION

117   **that pretty much says it all:** "Sen. Wyden Comments on Sens.
Wyden-Grassley-Inhofe-Salazar Amendment to End Secret Holds,"
U.S. Fed News Service, Including U.S. State News, March 29,
2006, HighBeam Research, http://www.highbeam.com/doc/1P3-
1014205011.html.

117   **eventually, the Senate did pass legislation:** Senator Ron Wyden,
"Wyden Amendment to End Secret Holds Approved by Senate,"
Press Release, December 6, 2006, http://wyden.senate.gov/
newsroom/press/release/?id=1c06be9d-2d08-49b3-9a58-
25bb76136d30.

118   **Senator Tom Harkin:** Senator Tom Harkin, "Remarks of Senator
Tom Harkin to the 2010 Living Constitution Lecture at the
Brennan Center for Justice," Press Release, June 15, 2010,
http://harkin.senate.gov/press/release.cfm?I-325688.

119   **donor networks:** Ezra Klein, "More Money, More Problems,"
Newsweek, October 31, 2010, www.newsweek.com/2010/10/31/
klein-money-politics-and-the-2010-midterms.html.

119   **high-dollar donors went on strike:** Ryan Grim, "Donor Strike:
Rich Progressives Pledge to Withhold Cash," Huffington Post, May
12, 2008, www.huffingtonpost.com/2010/05/12/donor-strike-rich-
progres_n_572766.html.

119   **I'd rather have campaign finance reform:** Quoted in Ryan Grim,
"Public Funding of Congressional Campaigns Widely Favored,"
Huffington Post, September 28, 2010, www.huffingtonpost.com/
2010/09/28/voters-favors-public-fund_n_742348.html.

119   **Change Congress:** Grim, "Donor Strike."

120   **Blue America:** Leslie Wayne, "A Fund-Raising Rainmaker
Arises Online," *New York Times*, November 26, 2007,
www.nytimes.com/2007/11/29/us/politics/29actblue
.html.

120   **companies to receive this resolution:** "Investors Announce
Challenges on Political Spending to Corporate Responsibility
Leaders: Role as U.S. Chamber of Commerce Board Members
Highlighted," Press Release, received by e-mail, November 4,
2010.

122 **leaving the United States alone:** Eric Alterman, *What Liberal Media? The Truth About Bias and the News* (New York: Basic Books, 2003), 26.

122 **congressional campaign financing reform:** Senate Majority Leader Robert Byrd, "Lobbyists," *U.S. Senate Legislations and Records*, September 28, 1987 (updated 1989), www.senate.gov/legislative/sommon/briefing/Byrd_History_Lobbying.htm.

122 **what legislators go through:** William Cohen, "A Look at the US Senate with William Cohen, George Packer, and Al Hunt," *Charlie Rose*, August 18, 2010, www.charlierose.com/view/interview/11173.

123 **2010 survey of freshman members:** James Hohmann and Alex Isenstadt, "Freshman Say Eric Massa Is Right About the Money," *Politico*, March 11, 2010, www.politico.com/news/stories/0310/34244.html.

123 **a tin cup in your hand:** Ezra Klein, "More Money, More Problems," *Newsweek*, October 31, 2010, www.newsweek.com/2010/10/31/klein-money-politics-and-the-2010-midterms.html.

123 **John Kerry's 2008 Massachusetts Senate race:** "Geography Data: 2008 Race: Massachusetts Senate; In-State vs. Out-of-State," OpenSecrets.org, www.opensecrets.org/races/geog.php?id=MAS2&cycle=2008.

123 **Fair Elections Now Act:** "H.R. 1826—Fair Elections Now Act," Open Congress, www.opencongress.org/bill/111-h1826/show.

124 **Fair Elections would be funded:** Sam Waterson, "Historic Movement on Fair Elections," Huffington Post, September 23, 2010, www.huffingtonpost.com/sam-waterston/historic-movement-on-fair_b_737084.html.

124 **those companies that wish to enjoy:** Trumka made these remarks on a panel, "Which Way for the Working Class: Elections 2010 and Beyond" sponsored by Working Families, AFL-CIO, on which he and the author appeared, the Great Hall, Cooper Union, New York City, September 24, 2010.

125 **when the top staffer:** Timothy P. Carney, "Former Barney Frank Staffer Now Top Goldman Sachs Lobbyist," *Washington Post*, April 28, 2009, www.washingtonexaminer.com/opinion/blogs/

beltway-confidential/Former-Barney-Frank-staffer-now-top-Goldman-Sachs-lobbyist-43914907.html#ixzz13UQssGef.

125   **Congress extended the break:** U.S. Congress, Senate, *Honest Leadership and Open Government Act of 2007*, 1st. sess., 110th Cong., http://thomas.loc.gov/cgi-bin/bdquery/z?d110:SN00001:@@@D&summ2=m&.

125   **Senator Trent Lott:** Martin Kady II and Josh Kraushaar, "Lott to Retire; Kyl Eyes Whip Role," *Politico*, November 26, 2007, www.politico.com/news/stories/1107/7032.html.

126   **Closing the Revolving Door Act:** U.S. Congress, Senate, *Close the Revolving Door Act of 2010*, S. 3272, 2nd sess.,111th Cong., http://thomas.loc.gov/cgi-bin/bdquery/z?d111:s3272.

126   **major liberal reforms require:** Harold Meyerson, "Without a Movement, Progressives Can't Aid Obama's Agenda," *Washington Post*, January 6, 2010, www.washingtonpost.com/wp-dyn/content/article/2010/01/05/AR2010010502989.html.

127   **movements had gestated for decades:** Michael Kazin, "Building a Movement by Offering Solutions," *The Nation*, August 12, 2010, www.thenation.com/article/154018/building-movement-offering-solutions.

127   **a conservative Republican in the presidency:** Conor Dougherty and Sara Murray "Lost Decade for Family Income," *Wall Street Journal*, September 17, 2010, http://online.wsj.com/article/SB10001434052748703440604575495670714069694.html.

127   **incomes fell 4.2 percent:** Ibid.

127   **even more amazing:** Ibid.

127   **gobble up nearly 24 percent:** Nichals D. Kristoff, "Our Banana Republic," *New York Times*, November 7, 21010, 10.

128   **John Judis and Ruy Teixeira predicted:** John B. Judis and Ruy Teixeira, "Back to the Future: The Re-emergence of the Emerging Democratic Majority," *American Prospect*, June 19, 2007, www.prospect.org/cs/articles?article=back_to_the_future061807.

129   **67 percent of the Hispanic vote:** Julia Preston, "In Big Shift, Latino Vote Was Heavily for Obama," *New York Times*, November 6, 2008, www.nytimes.com/2008/11/07/us/politics/07latino.html.

129   **anyone of Hispanic heritage:** Harry Reid, quoted in John McCormack, "Harry Reid: 'I Don't Know How Anyone of Hispanic Heritage Could Be a Republican,'" *Weekly Standard*, August 10, 2010, www.weeklystandard.com/blogs/harry-reid-i-dont-know-how-anyone-hispanic-heritage-could-be-republican.

131   **David Plouffe:** Lisa Taddeo, "The Man Who Made Obama," *Esquire*, November 3, 2009, www.esquire.com/features/david-plouffe-0309.

132   **to maintain the perception:** Micah L. Sifri, "The Obama Disconnect: What Happens When Myth Meets Reality," *Tech President*, December 31, 2009, http:/techpresident.com/blog-entry/the-obama-disconnect.

132   **primary challenges to sitting Democratic senators:** Ibid.

132   **looks less like a movement:** Charles Homans, "The Party of Obama: What Are the President's Grassroots Good For?" *Washington Monthly*, January–February 2010, www.washingtonmonthly.com/features/2010/1001.homans.html.

133   **Harbor Country Progress:** Jim Vopat, "Building the Left in Harbor Country," *In These Times*, September 30, 2009, www.inthesetimes.com/article/4913/building_the_left_in_harbor_country/.

133   **allows activists to maintain:** G. William Domhoff, "Leftists, Liberals—and Losers? How and Why Progressives Must Unite for Real Change," *In These Times,* December 21, 2009, www.inthesetimes.com/article/5314/leftists_liberalsand_losers/.

134   **failure to show up at the polls:** Norman Ornstein, "Ending the Permanent Campaign," *The Nation*, August 12, 2010, www.thenation.com/article/154016/ending-permanent-campaign.

134   **one survey of sixteen nations:** Jennifer S. Rosenberg with Margaret Chen, "Expanding Democracy: Voter Registration Around the World," Brennan Center for Justice at New York University School of Law, 2009, http://brennan.3cdn.net/3234b49c4234d92bf3_3km6i2ifu.pdf.

135   **Brennan Center for Legal Justice:** Wendy Weiser and Margaret Chen, "Can We Register to Vote Better? Yes," Brennan Center for Justice at New York University School of Law, July 10, 2009,

www.brennancenter.org/blog/archives.can_we_register_voters_
better_yes/.

135   **lose the right to vote for life:** "Overview and Summary Losing the
Vote: The Impact on Felony Disenfranchisement Laws in the
United States," Human Rights Watch: The Sentencing Project,
1998, www.hrw.org/reports98/vote/ndex.html#TopOfPage;
www.aclu.org/voting-rights/ex-offenders.

136   **differing state felony disfranchisement laws:** Robert Yoon, "CNN
Asks Florida Court for Ineligible Voters List," CNN, May 28, 2004,
http://articles.cnn.com/2004-05-28/politics/fla.vote_1_felon-list-
ineligible-voters-voter-rolls?_s=PM:ALLPOLITICS.

136   **Democracy Restoration Act:** U.S. Congress, Senate, *Democratic
Restoration Act of 2009*, S. 1516, 1st sess., 111th Cong.,
http://thomas.loc.gov/cgi-bin/query/z?c111:S.1516.

136   **just another household appliance:** Mark Fowler, cited in J. M.
Dempsey, "The Public Interest Must Dominate: Herbert Hoover
and Broadcasting's Public Interest Standard," Texas A&M
University, 2009.

137   **John Dewey and Walter Lippmann disagreed:** For additional
discussion of this debate, see Eric Alterman, *Sound and Fury: The
Making of the Punditocracy*, 2nd ed. (Ithaca, NY: Cornell University
Press, 1999) 287–289; Eric Alterman, *Who Speaks for America: Why
Democracy Matters in Foreign Policy* (Ithaca, NY: Cornell University
Press, 1998), 64–69, 153–155; Eric Alterman, *When Presidents Lie:
A History of Official Deception and Its Consequences* (New York:
Penguin, 2004) 310–314; and Eric Alterman, "Out of Print: The
Death and Life of the American Newspaper," *New Yorker*, March
31, 2008, www.newyorker.com/reporting/2008/03/.../080331fa_
fact_alterman.

139   **reporting less news in fewer pages:** Leonard Downie Jr. and
Michael Schudson, "Reconstruction of American Journalism,"
Columbia Journalism Review, October 19, 2009,
www.cjr.org/reconstruction/the_reconstruction_of_american.php.

139   **newsrooms have shrunk:** Project for Excellence in Journalism and
Rick Edmonds of the Poynter Institute, "Summary Essay," in *State*

of the News Media: An Annual Report on American Journalism,
www.stateofthemedia.org/2010/newspapers_summary_essay.php.

139   **increasingly on life support:** FCC Commissioner Michael J.
Copps, "Remarks to the Future of Media Workshop," *Public Interest
in the Digital Era,* March 4, 2010.

140   **taxpayer-funded high-quality journalism:** Downie and Schudson,
"Reconstruction of American Journalism."

140   **a similar fee in the United States:** Ibid.

141   **public radio and television:** Ibid.

141   **a national Fund for Local News:** Ibid.

141   **the annual ranking of The Economist:** Robert W. McChesney,
"Rejuvenating American Journalism: Some Tentative Policy
Proposals," Presentation to Workshop on Journalism Federal Trade
Commission, March 10, 2010, www.ftc.gov/opp/workshops/
news/mar9/docs/mcchesney.pdf.

142   **certain vital habits of democracy:** James W. Carey,
Communication as Culture: Essays on Media and Society (Boston:
Unwin Hyman, 1989), 79.

142   **a class of experts:** John Dewey, *The Public and Its Problems*
(New York: Henry Holt, 1927), 158.

143   **technology now with more power:** Copps, "Remarks."

143   **the quack, the charlatan:** Walter Lippmann, *Liberty and the News*
(New York: Harcourt, Brace and Howe, 1920), 54.

144   **to free the slaves:** Barack Obama, "Remarks by the President at the
DNC Gen44 Event," White House: Office of the Press Secretary,
October 1, 2010, www.whitehouse.gov/the-press-
office/2010/10/01/remarks-president-dnc-gen44-event.

EPILOGUE

145   **predicted a 45-seat loss:** Douglas Hibbs Jr., "The 2010
Midterm Election for the US House of Representatives," Center
for Public Sector Research Paper 9 (2010), http://douglas-
hibbs.com/house2010election22september2010.pdf. For useful
discussions of the Hibbs model and the Democrats' performance,
see Kevin Drum, "Chart of the Day: Democratic Losses in 2010,"
Mother Jones Online, October 29, 2010, http://motherjones.com/

kevin-drum/2010/10/chart-day-democratic-losses-2010; and Kevin Drum, "Two Lessons from the Election," *Mother Jones Online*, November 2, 2010, http://motherjones.com/kevin-drum/2010/11/two-lessons-election

145   **Republicans' best showing:** "Revolution in the States," *Wall Street Journal*, November 5, 2010, http://online.wsj.com/article/SB 10001424052748703506904575592570852081184.html?mod =googlenews_wsj.

145   **Democrats' worse performance:** Drum, "Two Lessons."

146   **communication was the one thing:** James Morone, quoted in Edward Luce, "Obama's Fearsome Foursome," *Financial Times*, February 6, 2010, http://www.businessspectator.com.au/bs.nsf/ Article/Obamas-fearsome-foursome-pd20100205-2D3U7?Open Document&src=sph.

146   **the worse recession:** Jann S. Wenner, "Obama in Command: The Rolling Stone Interview," *Rolling Stone Online*, September 28, 2010, www.rollingstone.com/politics/news/17390/209395?RS_show_page =0, 4000.

146   **preserve 3.7 million jobs:** Michael Leachman, "New CBO Report Finds Recovery Act Has Preserved or Created Up to 2.8 Million Jobs," May 26, 2010, Center on Budget and Policy Priorities, www.cbpp.org/cms/index.cfm?fa=view&id=3196.

146   **nearly $1,200:** Jeanne Sahadi, "Your Share of Stimulus Tax Breaks," CNNMoney.com, February 21, 2009, http://money.cnn.com/ 2009/02/21/news/economy/tax_savings_stimulus/index.htm.

146   **misimpression their tax bite:** Andy Barr, "Poll: Congress Did Less Than Usual," *Politico*, October 29, 2010, http://dyn.politico .com/printstory.cfm?uuid=F7EE874E-92C1-6978-862161837F5 FB23B; Michael Cooper, "From Obama, the Tax Cut Nobody Heard Of," *New York Times*, October 18, 2010, www.nytimes.com/ 2010/10/19/us/politics/19taxes.html?_r=1&scp=1&sq=poll,%20tax %20cut,%20&st=cse.

146   **favored the repeal:** Bloomberg National Poll, Study #1999, October 7–10, 2010, www.scribd.com/doc/39289347/Bloomberg-Survey.

147   **unemployment is still bad:** Steven Greenhouse, "Unions Find Members Slow to Rally Behind Democrats," *New York Times*,

September 17, 2010,
www.nytimes.com/2010/09/18/us/181abor.html.

147   **Obama's supermajority:** Eugene Goodhart, "Obama On and Off
       Base," *Dissent*, Summer 2010,
       www.dissentmagazine.org/article/?article=3268.

147   **perverse pride:** Peter Baker, "Education of a President," *New York
       Times Magazine*, October 12, 2010, MM40.

148   **foreclosure on their homes:** See James K. Galbraith, "Obama's
       Problem Simply Defined: It Was the Banks," new deal 2.0,
       November 5, 2010, www.newdeal20.org/2010/11/05/obamas-
       problem-simply-defined-it-was-the-banks-26159/. For more on the
       underlying argument, see John Maynard Keynes, "The
       Consequences to the Banks of the Collapse of Money Values," in
       Essays in Persuasion (New York: Norton, 1991).

149   **$30,000 per person:** Eric Alterman, "How Obama Screws His
       Base," *Daily Beast*, September 19, 2010, www.thedailybeast.com/
       blogs-and-stories/2010-09-19/how-obama-screws-his-liberal-
       base/2/.

149   **as though we are children:** Luce, "Obama's Fearsome Foursome."

150   **err on the side of too much:** Paul Krugman, "Franklin Delano
       Obama," *New York Times*, November 10, 2008,
       www.nytimes.com/2008/11/10/opinion/10krugman.html?scp=1&s
       q=krugman,%20november%2010,%202008&st=cse.

151   **a genuine recovery:** Ryan Lizza, "Inside the Crisis," *New Yorker*,
       October 12, 2009, www.newyorker.com/reporting/2009/10/
       12/091012fa_fact_lizza.

151   **in the art of the possible:** Ryan Lizza, "The Gatekeeper," *New
       Yorker*, March 2, 2009, www.newyorker.com/reporting/2009/03/
       02/090302fa_fact_lizza?currentPage=all.

152   **indigenous American beserk:** Roth coined this term in his novel
       American Pastoral, for which he won the 1998 Pulitzer Prize for
       fiction. Obama was elected the first black president of the *Harvard
       Law Review* in February 1990. See Fox Butterfield, "First Black
       Elected to Head Harvard's Law Review," *New York Times*, February
       6, 1990, www.nytimes.com/1990/02/06/us/first-black-elected-to-
       head-harvard-s-law-review.html.

152   **a one-term president:** Michael A. Memoli, "Mitch McConnell's Remarks on 2012 Draw White House Irc," *Los Angeles Times*, October 27, 2010, http://articles.latimes.com/2010/oct/27/news/la-pn-obama-mcconnell-20101027.

152   **a mantle of moral leadership:** Marshall Ganz, "How Obama Lost His Voice, and How He Can Get It Back," *Los Angeles Times*, November 3, 2010, http://articles.latimes.com/2010/nov/03/opinion/la-oe-1103-ganz-obama-20101103.

153   **transformational leadership:** Ibid.

153   **abandoned the bully pulpit:** ibid.

154   **averting a far greater catastrophe:** Thomas E. Mann, "American Politics on the Eve of the Midterm Elections," Chatham House, October 2010.

154   **the youth vote:** Ruy Teixeira and John Halpin, "Election Results Fueled by Jobs Crisis and Voter Apathy Among Progressives," Center for American Progress Action Fund, November 4, 2010, www.americanprogressaction.org/issues/2010/11/election_a-nalysis.html.

155   **this was the moment:** Barack Obama, "America, This Is Our Moment," YouTube, June 4, 2008, www.youtube.com/watch?v=kbbIQFcEhcQ.

158   **all that soul:** Adele M. Stan, "Van Jones: We Must Prepare for Battle," Alternet, November 6, 2010, www.alternet.org/news/148764/van_jones:_we_must_prepare_for_battle/?page=entire.

ACKNOWLEDGMENTS

Books, I am hardly the first person to point out, have individual authors but represent the collective efforts of large teams of people. First off, thanks to Ari Melber for drafting the section of the Conclusion dealing with legislative and campaign finance reform. I want to thank my editor, Ruth Baldwin, and everyone at Nation Books and Perseus Books. So, too, Taya Kitman, Andy Breslau, and the staff of the Nation Institute. At the *Nation* magazine, my considerable gratitude belongs to my editors Betsy Reed (who edited the original essay upon which this book was based) and Katrina vanden Heuvel, as well as to the many interns who helped with the fact-checking and footnoting. These include Devon Bancroft, Laurie Rojas, Hayes Clark, Neima Jahromi, Marissa Colon-Margolies, and Carrie Battan. Thanks also to Kate Murphy, who helped to coordinate the interns. Tina Bennett, once again, was the agent to end all agents. Thanks to her and Svetlana Katz. The book version of this essay also benefited greatly from the scholars who responded to the original version. These include Barbara Ehrenreich, Norman Ornstein, Michael Kazin, Chris Bowers, Salim Muwakkil, and Theda Skocpol. Thanks also go to Mike Allen of *Politico* and Neera Tanden of the Center for American Progress for their helpful responses to the original. Other friends and colleagues who helped give life to and/or sustain my work on this project include Victor Navasky, Bill Moyers, Rick Kot, Laura Tisdel, Ellen Tremper, Danny Goldberg, the crack editorial team at the Center for American Progress, *Moment* magazine, the *Daily Beast*, my colleagues at the Brooklyn College English Department and the CUNY Graduate

School of Journalism, and, most of all, my readers at all those places. Finally, thanks also to my family, Diana Silver and Eve Rose Alterman, and my parents, Carl and Ruth Alterman, for (almost) all they do, did, and will do in the future.

INDEX

Abercrombie, Neil, 19
Abramoff, Jack, 15
Abramson, Jill, 103
ACORN (Association of Community Organizations for Reform Now), 54, 100–106, 107
ActBlue, 120
Adler, Ivan H., 56
Afghanistan, 11, 23, 112
AIG, 46, 51, 110
Ajami, Fouad, 89–90
al Qaida, 40, 81
Alexander, Andrew, 103
Allen, Mike, 55, 112
American Action Network, 64
American Enterprise Institute, 24, 44, 97, 134
American Future Fund (AFF), 71–72
American Journalism Review, 10, 11
Americans for Prosperity Foundation, 71
Angle, Sharron, 77–78, 83
Antigovernment ideology; and corporations, conservatives, and the wealthy, 32, 66–70; and Obama's agenda, 70; and Paine and Thoreau, 65; and Pew poll, 66; and regulation, 16; and Republicans, 18, 65
Armey, Dick, 54, 71
Atlantic Monthly, 3
Automobile companies, 49, 146
Axelrod, David, 98

Baker, Peter, 147
"Balloon Boy" hoax, 112
Bankruptcies, 8
Banks; and bailouts and TARP, 9, 25, 46, 50; and executive pay, 50–51; and lobbying, 47, 48, 49, 54–59; and

Obama's advisers, 148; and regulation and reform, 46–54, 60; and Schumer, 59–61; *See also* Financial industry
Barbour, Haley, 92, 93
Bartlett, Bruce, 70
Bartley, Robert, 66
Bartlit, Fred H., Jr., 14
Baumgartner, Frank, 35–36
Bayh, Evan, 123
Beck, Glenn, 107; and ACORN, 101, 102; and global warming, 43; on Obama, 84, 85, 86; and Rauf, 81; on Soros, 86–87; and Tea Party, 87; and Tides Center, 85–86; and violent fear-mongering, 86
Bennahum, David, 139
Bennet, Michael, 126
Berlusconi, Silvio, 79
Bernanke, Ben, 53, 68, 148
Bersin, Alan, 30
Beyoncé, 158
Bilmes, Linda J., 8
bin Talal, Prince Alwaleed, 82
Black, William K., 53
Blue America, 120
Blumenthal, Paul, 33
Boehlert, Erich, 85
Boehner, John, 21, 56
Bogle, John C., 61
Bolton, Susan, 92
Bono, 158
Boudreau, Abbie, 107
BP oil spill, 11–16, 37, 55, 110–111
Bradley, Bill, 113
Brauchli, Marcus, 103
Breitbart, Andrew, 101–102, 106, 107, 114
Briggs, Dave, 88

ABOUT THE AUTHOR

ERIC ALTERMAN is a Distinguished Professor of English and Journalism at Brooklyn College, City University of New York, and a Professor of Journalism at the CUNY Graduate School of Journalism. He is also "The Liberal Media" columnist for *The Nation* and a fellow of the Nation Institute; a senior fellow at the Center for American Progress in Washington, DC, where he writes the "Think Again" column; and a senior fellow (since 1985) at the World Policy Institute. Alterman is also a columnist on Jewish issues for *Moment* magazine and on politics for the "Daily Beast." He is the author of seven earlier books, including the national best-sellers *What Liberal Media? The Truth About Bias and the News* (2003, 2004), and *The Book on Bush: How George W. (Mis)leads America* (2004, 2005). The others include *When Presidents Lie: A History of Official Deception and Its Consequences* (2004, 2005); *Sound and Fury: The Making of the Punditocracy* (1992, 2000), winner of the 1992 George Orwell Award; *It Ain't No Sin to Be Glad You're Alive: The Promise of Bruce Springsteen* (1999, 2001), winner of the 1999 Stephen Crane Literary Award; *Who Speaks for America? Why Democracy Matters in Foreign Policy* (1998); and *Why We're Liberals: A Handbook for Restoring America's Most Important Ideals* (2008, 2009). A graduate of Cornell, Yale, and Stanford universities, he lives in Manhattan with his family.